THE GOOD ENERGY COOKBOOK

Boost Your Energy All Day Long with 100+ Nourishing Recipes Inspired by Dr. Casey Means' Teachings for Sustained Vitality and Wellness.

Sophia Köhler

INSIDE THE BOOK

EXCLUSIVE BONUSES!

HIGH-ENERGY WORK MEAL PLAN

POST-WORKOUT MEAL PLAN

SIMPLE DETOX MEAL PLAN

SCROLL TO THE END AND
SCAN THE **QR-CODE**

TABLE OF CONTENTS

Introduction: The Power of Food for Lasting Energy

What is a Good Energy Diet?

Do you ever find yourself reaching for that afternoon coffee, hoping it will get you through the rest of the day, only to feel drained an hour later? Or maybe you've experienced that post-lunch slump that makes it hard to focus or stay productive. These are signs that your body isn't getting the sustained energy it needs from your meals. This is where the **Good Energy Diet** comes in.

A Good Energy Diet isn't about restricting calories or following the latest food trends. It's about eating balanced, nutrient-dense meals that keep your energy levels steady throughout the day. The right foods can fuel your body like a well-oiled machine, giving you the stamina and focus you need for everything from tackling your to-do list to crushing your workouts.

At its core, the Good Energy Diet focuses on providing your body with the **right balance of macronutrients—** proteins, healthy fats, and complex carbohydrates—to sustain your energy, avoid blood sugar spikes and crashes, and keep you feeling alert and refreshed. It's not about quick fixes or energy drinks. Instead, it emphasizes whole, unprocessed foods that nourish your body from the inside out, providing lasting vitality.

By incorporating foods that digest slowly, you give your body a steady supply of fuel. Complex carbs like whole grains, fiber-rich vegetables, lean proteins, and healthy fats all play a key role in maintaining stable energy levels. These foods also help regulate blood sugar, improve digestion, and keep you feeling satisfied longer, reducing cravings and mood swings.

The Good Energy Diet isn't just about avoiding certain foods—it's about **choosing the right ones**. Foods high in refined sugar, unhealthy fats, and processed carbs may provide a quick energy boost, but they lead to rapid energy drops, leaving you feeling sluggish and craving more. Instead, this diet encourages you to fill your plate with vibrant, nutrient-dense options that power your body in a way that makes you feel good, not just for an hour, but all day long. From breakfast to dinner, and even those mid-day snacks, every meal can be an opportunity to fuel your body for lasting energy. Let's explore how to take control of your energy through the meals you eat.

The Importance of Sustained Energy

In our fast-paced lives, energy isn't just a nice-to-have; it's essential. Whether you're navigating a busy workday, keeping up with family demands, or fitting in that workout, sustained energy is the key to performing at your best, both mentally and physically. But why is sustained energy so important, and why do we often struggle to maintain it throughout the day?

When we talk about sustained energy, we're talking about the ability to feel consistently alert, focused, and active, without experiencing energy crashes or fatigue. Unlike short-term energy boosts that come from quick fixes like caffeine or sugary snacks, sustained energy is steady and long-lasting, powered by the right foods that give your body exactly what it needs to function efficiently.

Without sustained energy, it's easy to fall into the cycle of ups and downs. You might start the day feeling good, but by mid-morning or mid-afternoon, you're sluggish, unfocused, and reaching for anything that promises a fast pick-me-up. This rollercoaster of energy is often caused by unbalanced meals or poor food choices, leading to blood sugar spikes and rapid drops that leave you exhausted.

Maintaining sustained energy has a profound impact on your productivity, mood, and health:

- **Improved Mental Clarity**: When your energy is balanced, so is your ability to think clearly and stay focused. You can make better decisions, stay creative, and tackle your tasks efficiently without feeling mentally drained.
- **Increased Physical Stamina**: Whether you're working out or simply getting through a busy day, sustained energy helps you maintain strength and endurance. It allows your body to perform at its peak without feeling fatigued or weak.
- **Stable Mood**: Have you ever felt irritable or anxious after a sugar crash? The food you eat directly affects your mood. By fuelling your body with the right nutrients, you can avoid mood swings and feel more balanced throughout the day.
- **Better Sleep**: Surprisingly, the food you eat during the day can impact how well you sleep at night. A diet that supports sustained energy helps regulate your body's natural rhythms, making it easier to wind down and enjoy restful sleep.
- **Long-Term Health Benefits**: Eating for sustained energy supports your overall health. Balanced meals rich in whole foods contribute to a healthy metabolism, better digestion, and a lower risk of chronic illnesses such as diabetes and heart disease.

Your body is constantly working to keep your energy levels stable. However, when we fuel it with poor food choices—highly processed meals, refined sugars, and unhealthy fats—it has to work overtime, leading to spikes in energy followed by sudden crashes. These crashes don't just affect how you feel; they impact your productivity, motivation, and even your long-term health.

Sustained energy is the foundation of a healthy, balanced life. By focusing on whole, nutrient-dense foods that provide long-lasting fuel, you give your body the support it needs to power through your day without hitting that wall of exhaustion. You can be more productive at work, more present with your family, and more energized during your workouts—all without relying on temporary fixes.

In this book, you'll learn how to build a diet that promotes sustained energy, keeping you energized and focused from morning until night. Let's dive into how you can make simple changes to your meals to unlock steady, lasting energy throughout your day.

Benefits of a Good Energy Diet

Imagine feeling energized from the moment you wake up until the end of the day, without the usual dips in focus or that dreaded mid-afternoon slump. This is the power of a **Good Energy Diet**, a way of eating that not only fuels your body but also sustains your energy levels throughout the day. But what exactly are the benefits of following this approach, and how can it transform your life?

Let's explore the key benefits of adopting a Good Energy Diet:

1. Consistent Energy Levels

One of the biggest advantages of a Good Energy Diet is the ability to maintain steady energy throughout the day. By eating balanced meals that combine protein, healthy fats, and complex carbohydrates, you avoid the spikes and crashes caused by sugary or processed foods. Instead of quick bursts of energy followed by fatigue, you experience a slow, steady release of fuel that keeps you going longer. This means no more dragging yourself through the afternoon, struggling to stay awake, or relying on caffeine to get you through the day.

2. Enhanced Mental Clarity and Focus

The brain requires a constant supply of nutrients to function at its best. When your diet is unbalanced or full of quick-burning sugars, your concentration suffers. A Good Energy Diet helps stabilize blood sugar levels, which in turn improves mental clarity, memory, and focus. Whether you're tackling a project at work, studying, or managing your daily tasks, the right food choices can sharpen your thinking and keep you productive for longer periods without the fogginess or distraction that often accompanies energy dips.

3. Better Physical Performance

Whether you're an athlete, a gym-goer, or simply active in your daily life, sustained energy is essential for physical performance. A Good Energy Diet provides the nutrients your muscles need to function efficiently and recover quickly. Complex carbs fuel your workouts, proteins repair and strengthen your muscles, and healthy fats keep your body functioning optimally. With the right balance of these nutrients, you'll experience improved stamina, strength, and endurance, whether you're at the gym or simply staying active throughout the day.

4. Stable Mood and Emotional Balance

The foods we eat have a profound impact on our mood. Processed sugars and refined carbs can cause drastic blood sugar fluctuations, leading to irritability, anxiety, and even mood swings. In contrast, a Good Energy Diet helps keep your blood sugar levels stable, which directly influences your emotional well-being. You'll experience fewer highs and lows, staying emotionally balanced and resilient throughout the day. This can improve your relationships, your ability to handle stress, and your overall sense of well-being.

5. Support for Healthy Weight Management

A Good Energy Diet is naturally aligned with healthy weight management. By focusing on whole, nutrient-dense foods that keep you full longer, you avoid the cravings and overeating that come with processed, low-nutrient foods. The balance of fiber, protein, and healthy fats helps regulate appetite and keeps you satisfied between meals, making it easier to maintain or reach your ideal weight without feeling deprived or hungry.

6. Improved Sleep Quality

Believe it or not, the food you eat during the day can significantly impact how well you sleep at night. A diet rich in whole foods and balanced nutrients helps regulate your body's circadian rhythm, making it easier for you to wind down at night and enjoy deeper, more restful sleep. Foods high in vitamins and minerals, such as magnesium and potassium, also help relax the body and reduce stress, setting you up for a good night's rest.

7. Long-Term Health and Vitality

The benefits of a Good Energy Diet extend far beyond short-term gains. Over time, eating this way can lead to better overall health, reducing the risk of chronic conditions such as heart disease, diabetes, and inflammation. Whole, nutrient-rich foods contain antioxidants, vitamins, and minerals that support everything from your immune system to your skin's appearance. This way of eating promotes long-term vitality, helping you live a more active, healthy, and fulfilling life.

By embracing a Good Energy Diet, you are investing in your long-term health, performance, and overall happiness. From improving your daily focus and physical stamina to balancing your mood and supporting your long-term wellness, the benefits of eating for energy are far-reaching. The meals in this book are designed to help you unlock the full potential of your body and mind—giving you the sustained energy you need to thrive every single day.

Now that we've explored the benefits, let's dive into the foods that will help you achieve this lasting energy and learn which ones to avoid for optimal results.

Foods to Include for Lasting Energy

These are the foods that provide a steady, long-lasting energy supply to your body and brain, ensuring you stay fueled throughout the day:

1. **Complex Carbohydrates**
   o **Examples**: Oats, quinoa, brown rice, sweet potatoes, whole-grain bread, legumes
   o **Why Include**: Complex carbs are rich in fiber, which slows digestion and provides a gradual release of energy. They help stabilize blood sugar levels and keep you feeling full longer, preventing energy crashes.
2. **Lean Proteins**
   o **Examples**: Chicken, turkey, eggs, fish, Greek yogurt, tofu, lentils, beans

- o **Why Include**: Protein is essential for repairing tissues, maintaining muscle mass, and stabilizing energy levels. It helps keep you full and satisfied, while also supporting metabolism and muscle function.
3. **Healthy Fats**
    - o **Examples**: Avocados, olive oil, nuts, seeds, fatty fish (salmon, mackerel), coconut oil
    - o **Why Include**: Healthy fats are an excellent source of sustained energy. They provide essential fatty acids that support brain health and cellular function, and help with the absorption of fat-soluble vitamins like A, D, E, and K.
4. **Fiber-Rich Vegetables**
    - o **Examples**: Spinach, kale, broccoli, Brussels sprouts, carrots, bell peppers
    - o **Why Include**: Vegetables high in fiber help slow the absorption of sugar into the bloodstream, preventing energy spikes and crashes. They are also packed with vitamins and minerals that support overall health and vitality.
5. **Low-Glycemic Fruits**
    - o **Examples**: Berries (blueberries, strawberries), apples, pears, cherries, citrus fruits
    - o **Why Include**: Low-glycemic fruits contain natural sugars that are slowly digested, preventing rapid spikes in blood sugar. They are also high in antioxidants and vitamins, which support immune function and overall well-being.
6. **Whole Grains**
    - o **Examples**: Brown rice, whole wheat pasta, barley, farro, bulgur
    - o **Why Include**: Whole grains provide complex carbohydrates, fiber, and essential nutrients like B vitamins, which are important for energy metabolism. They offer a steady source of fuel that can keep you energized for hours.
7. **Hydrating Foods**
    - o **Examples**: Cucumbers, watermelon, celery, leafy greens, citrus fruits
    - o **Why Include**: Staying hydrated is crucial for maintaining energy. Foods with high water content help keep your body hydrated, support digestion, and boost mental clarity throughout the day.

Foods to Avoid for Sustained Energy

These foods can lead to rapid spikes in energy followed by crashes, leaving you feeling sluggish, tired, and unable to focus. Limiting or avoiding these items can help keep your energy steady:

1. **Refined Sugars**
    - o **Examples**: Candy, soda, pastries, sugary cereals, packaged desserts
    - o **Why Avoid**: Refined sugars provide a quick but temporary energy boost by spiking blood sugar levels. This is often followed by a sharp drop in energy, leading to fatigue and cravings for more sugar.
2. **Refined Carbohydrates**
    - o **Examples**: White bread, white pasta, white rice, pastries, cookies
    - o **Why Avoid**: Like refined sugars, refined carbs are stripped of their fiber and nutrients, causing them to be digested quickly. This leads to energy crashes, increased hunger, and difficulty maintaining stable blood sugar levels.
3. **Highly Processed Foods**
    - o **Examples**: Fast food, pre-packaged snacks, frozen meals, chips

o **Why Avoid**: Processed foods are often loaded with unhealthy fats, added sugars, and artificial ingredients. They provide little nutritional value and can contribute to inflammation, digestive issues, and fluctuating energy levels.

4. **Sugary Beverages**
   o **Examples**: Soda, energy drinks, sugary coffee drinks, sweetened juices
   o **Why Avoid**: Sugary drinks can lead to rapid spikes in blood sugar followed by an energy crash. They also offer empty calories with little to no nutritional benefit, leading to dehydration and further fatigue.

5. **Trans Fats and Unhealthy Fats**
   o **Examples**: Fried foods, margarine, commercially baked goods (cakes, cookies), packaged snacks
   o **Why Avoid**: Trans fats and unhealthy saturated fats can increase inflammation, slow digestion, and make you feel sluggish. They offer no lasting energy benefits and are linked to various health issues, including heart disease.

6. **Excessive Caffeine**
   o **Examples**: Coffee, energy drinks, caffeinated sodas
   o **Why Avoid**: While moderate caffeine intake can provide a temporary energy boost, excessive caffeine leads to jitteriness, dehydration, and a crash in energy levels later. It can also interfere with sleep, causing long-term energy depletion.

7. **Alcohol**
   o **Examples**: Beer, wine, spirits
   o **Why Avoid**: Alcohol is a depressant that slows the central nervous system. It can cause drowsiness, dehydration, and disrupt sleep, all of which lead to low energy the following day.

The key to maintaining lasting energy throughout the day is choosing foods that nourish your body while avoiding those that sap your energy. By incorporating complex carbohydrates, lean proteins, healthy fats, fiber-rich vegetables, and hydrating foods, you can keep your energy levels steady and your mind sharp. At the same time, limiting refined sugars, processed foods, and unhealthy fats will help you avoid the crashes and fatigue that come with poor food choices.

In the following chapters, you'll discover how to build delicious, energizing meals using these foods, so you can feel your best from morning to night. Let's dive into the recipes that will transform the way you eat and fuel your body!

Chapter 1: The Science Behind Energizing Foods

Understanding the Science

When it comes to maintaining lasting energy throughout the day, the science of nutrition plays a critical role. The types of foods we eat directly affect how our bodies produce and use energy. While some foods provide quick bursts of energy that rapidly fade, others are designed to fuel our bodies for longer periods, ensuring that we feel energized and focused without the dips and crashes. To understand how to harness the power of energizing foods, it's important to look at the role of complex carbohydrates, healthy fats, and lean proteins and how they interact with your body's energy systems.

Blood Sugar Regulation: The Key to Steady Energy

At the heart of maintaining steady energy levels is blood sugar regulation. When we eat, our bodies convert carbohydrates into glucose, which is used as a primary source of energy. However, not all carbohydrates are created equal. Foods high in refined sugars and simple carbohydrates, such as candy or white bread, cause rapid spikes in blood sugar, followed by sharp drops. This quick rise and fall leave you feeling energized for a short time, but soon after, you experience an energy crash, fatigue, and cravings for more sugary foods.

In contrast, complex carbohydrates, such as whole grains, sweet potatoes, and legumes, are digested more slowly. They provide a gradual release of glucose into the bloodstream, keeping your energy levels more stable. These foods are rich in fiber, which slows the digestive process, preventing the rapid spikes and crashes associated with simple carbs. By choosing complex carbohydrates, you help your body maintain balanced blood sugar levels, which translates into more consistent energy throughout the day.

Slow-Digesting Nutrients for Long-Lasting Energy

Foods that digest slowly—like those rich in fiber, healthy fats, and proteins—play a key role in providing lasting energy. Here's how each of these nutrients contributes to sustained vitality:

1. Complex Carbohydrates

- How They Work: Complex carbs are made up of longer chains of sugar molecules, which take longer for the body to break down and convert into glucose. Because of this slow digestion, complex carbs provide a steady and reliable source of energy over a longer period. They also help keep blood sugar levels stable, reducing the likelihood of energy crashes.

- Examples: Brown rice, oats, quinoa, whole wheat bread, and legumes.

2. Healthy Fats

- How They Work: Unlike carbohydrates, fats provide a more concentrated source of energy. Healthy fats, such as those found in avocados, nuts, seeds, and fatty fish, are digested slowly, making them an excellent source of sustained energy. Fats take longer to break down, which helps keep you fuller for longer and provides a steady stream of energy without causing blood sugar fluctuations.
- Examples: Avocado, olive oil, nuts, seeds, and fatty fish like salmon and mackerel.

3. Lean Proteins

- How They Work: Proteins are essential for muscle repair, tissue health, and overall body function. While protein itself is not a primary energy source, it plays an important role in keeping you energized by supporting muscle recovery, curbing hunger, and stabilizing blood sugar. Lean proteins are digested more slowly than carbohydrates, helping prevent hunger and energy dips.
- Examples: Chicken, turkey, fish, eggs, tofu, and legumes.

Impact on Mental Clarity and Focus

The food we eat doesn't just affect our physical energy—it also has a direct impact on our mental performance. Certain nutrients, particularly those found in complex carbohydrates and healthy fats, provide essential fuel for the brain. Glucose is the brain's primary source of energy, and when blood sugar levels are stable, it allows for sharper focus, clearer thinking, and improved memory.

On the other hand, when you consume simple carbs and refined sugars, the rapid rise and fall of blood sugar can lead to brain fog, difficulty concentrating, and mood swings. This is why foods that stabilize blood sugar—like complex carbs, proteins, and healthy fats—are critical for maintaining mental clarity throughout the day.

Healthy fats, especially omega-3 fatty acids found in fish and flaxseeds, also play an important role in brain function. These fats support cognitive health, reduce inflammation, and help improve mood and focus, making them essential for both physical and mental energy.

The Power of Combining Nutrients

One of the most effective strategies for sustained energy is combining different macronutrients in every meal. When you pair complex carbs with lean proteins and healthy fats, you create a meal that is digested at a slower rate, providing a steady supply of energy over several hours. This balance helps you avoid energy spikes and crashes, while also keeping you satisfied longer, reducing cravings for sugary or processed foods.

For example, a meal like grilled chicken with quinoa and roasted vegetables combines all three macronutrients: the quinoa provides complex carbs for steady energy, the chicken offers lean protein for muscle support, and the olive oil used for roasting adds healthy fats that slow digestion and provide long-lasting fuel.

Fuelling for Lasting Energy

Understanding the science behind energizing foods empowers you to make smarter dietary choices that directly impact your energy levels, focus, and overall well-being. By choosing slow-digesting, nutrient-dense foods like complex carbohydrates, healthy fats, and lean proteins, you can regulate your blood sugar levels, improve mental clarity, and stay fuelled throughout the day. These small but powerful changes can transform the way you feel and perform, giving you the sustained energy you need to thrive—both physically and mentally.

In the next chapters, you'll find recipes that incorporate these key foods, helping you easily apply the science of nutrition to your everyday meals. Let's start building your good energy diet!

Chapter 2: Nutritional Information & Tips

Understanding the Power of Nutritional Information

When it comes to eating for sustained energy, understanding the nutritional breakdown of your meals can make all the difference. The foods you eat contain a variety of nutrients that fuel your body in different ways, and knowing how to read and apply nutritional information helps you make smarter choices that keep your energy levels stable and your body well-nourished.

In this chapter, we'll explore why nutritional information is key to maintaining energy, how to interpret and use the data provided with each recipe, and how you can tailor your meals to meet your specific energy and fitness goals.

The Role of Key Nutrients in Sustained Energy

To keep your energy levels steady throughout the day, it's important to focus on three macronutrients: carbohydrates, proteins, and fats. These macronutrients work together to fuel your body, and the balance of these nutrients in each meal will determine how long your energy lasts.

- **Carbohydrates:** The body's main source of energy. Choose complex carbs (whole grains, vegetables, legumes) for slow, steady energy release. These help maintain stable blood sugar levels, avoiding spikes and crashes.
- **Proteins:** Essential for muscle repair and satiety. Proteins digest slowly and help maintain steady energy levels by preventing hunger. They also play a role in muscle recovery and metabolic health.
- **Fats:** Healthy fats (avocados, nuts, seeds, olive oil) provide long-lasting energy because they take longer to digest. They also support brain function, helping you stay mentally sharp and focused.

Each recipe in this book is designed to provide a balanced combination of these macronutrients to support your energy needs.

How to Read Nutritional Information

For each recipe in this book, you'll find a breakdown of the key nutritional values, including:

- **Calories:** This is the total energy your body will get from the meal. Depending on your activity level and goals, you can adjust portion sizes to match your calorie needs.

- **Carbohydrates:** The amount of carbs in a meal will influence how quickly your body uses energy. Complex carbohydrates are essential for sustained energy, while lower-carb options may be better suited to those following a low-carb or ketogenic diet.
- **Protein:** Protein is crucial for maintaining muscle mass, supporting recovery, and keeping you feeling full. Each recipe provides a good balance of protein to keep your energy levels steady.
- **Fats:** Healthy fats not only provide energy but also help absorb fat-soluble vitamins (A, D, E, K). The fat content of each meal is carefully balanced to promote optimal energy and brain function.
- **Fiber:** Fiber helps slow digestion, which contributes to the steady release of energy. High-fiber meals keep you fuller longer and support digestive health, preventing energy dips caused by rapid digestion.

Customizing Nutritional Intake for Your Goals

Whether your goal is to boost energy, support fitness performance, or maintain a healthy weight, knowing how to use nutritional information is crucial. Here are some tips to help you tailor your meals based on your personal needs:

1. Adjust Portion Sizes Based on Activity Level

- If you're highly active or training for endurance, you may need larger portions or higher-calorie meals. Add extra complex carbs like whole grains or starchy vegetables for more sustained energy.
- If you're aiming for weight maintenance or weight loss, opt for slightly smaller portions or focus on protein and fiber-rich meals to help keep you full while managing calorie intake.

2. Focus on Protein for Recovery and Muscle Support

- For those looking to build or maintain muscle mass, aim to increase your protein intake. You can add more lean protein to any meal by including additional chicken, fish, tofu, or plant-based proteins like beans or lentils.

3. Choose Healthy Fats for Brain Power and Satiety

- If you find yourself needing longer-lasting energy or greater mental focus, slightly increase your intake of healthy fats. A handful of nuts, a spoonful of avocado, or a drizzle of olive oil can help extend the energy life of your meals.

4. Keep Fiber High for Steady Digestion

- Fiber plays a key role in regulating digestion and energy release. Opt for fiber-rich vegetables, legumes, and whole grains in every meal to slow digestion and keep blood sugar stable, reducing the chances of a post-meal crash.

Meal Timing for Optimal Energy

Along with understanding the nutritional makeup of your meals, when you eat also plays a role in maintaining energy. Here are some practical tips for timing your meals:

- **Start Your Day Right:** Begin with a protein- and fiber-rich breakfast to set the tone for balanced energy. Skipping breakfast or choosing sugary options can lead to energy dips later in the day.
- **Snack Smart:** Healthy snacks between meals, such as a handful of nuts or a piece of fruit, can help bridge the gap between meals and keep energy steady.
- **Pre-Workout Fuel:** If you exercise regularly, focus on a meal or snack with complex carbs and a bit of protein an hour or two before your workout. This will give you the energy needed for optimal performance.
- **Post-Workout Recovery:** After exercise, replenish your energy stores with a meal that includes protein for muscle recovery and complex carbs to restore glycogen levels.

Tracking Your Energy-Boosting Diet

To get the most out of your Good Energy Diet, it's helpful to track how different meals make you feel. Pay attention to how your body reacts to different foods and adjust as needed. You may find that certain meals leave you feeling more energized, while others might make you feel sluggish. This awareness will help you refine your eating habits and create a diet that works best for your body.

Making Nutritional Information Work for You

By understanding and using the nutritional information in this book, you can take full control of your energy levels, fitness goals, and overall well-being. Each recipe provides a balance of macronutrients designed to support sustained energy, allowing you to customize your meals based on your needs. Whether you're looking to boost your stamina, improve mental clarity, or simply feel better throughout the day, mastering the science of nutrition will empower you to thrive with every meal.

Chapter 3: Breakfast for Sustained Energy

Breakfast is often referred to as the most important meal of the day—and for good reason. It sets the tone for your energy levels, mood, and focus for the hours to come. When you start your day with a balanced, nutrient-dense breakfast, you're giving your body the fuel it needs to power through the morning without crashing or relying on caffeine or sugary snacks. A well-designed breakfast provides sustained energy, helping you avoid that mid-morning slump and keeping you feeling satisfied until your next meal.

Why Breakfast Matters for Energy

Your body fasts overnight while you sleep, using stored energy to maintain essential functions. When you wake up, those energy stores are low, and your body needs replenishment. Skipping breakfast or opting for foods that are high in refined sugars can lead to quick bursts of energy followed by rapid crashes, leaving you feeling tired and sluggish long before lunchtime.

By choosing a breakfast rich in **complex carbohydrates, lean proteins, and healthy fats**, you'll create a steady source of fuel that helps regulate blood sugar levels, keeping you focused and energized. These macronutrients work together to provide a balanced release of energy over several hours, making sure you feel alert, full, and ready to tackle whatever the day throws at you.

Key Ingredients for an Energizing Breakfast

To build a breakfast that supports sustained energy, focus on these key components:

1. **Complex Carbohydrates**
   o **Why**: These slow-digesting carbs are your body's primary energy source. Unlike simple carbs, which cause blood sugar spikes and crashes, complex carbs provide a steady release of glucose into your bloodstream.
   o **Examples**: Oats, whole-grain bread, quinoa, sweet potatoes, and whole-grain cereals.
2. **Lean Proteins**
   o **Why**: Protein helps keep you feeling full and supports muscle repair and growth. It also stabilizes blood sugar, ensuring a balanced energy release throughout the morning.
   o **Examples**: Eggs, Greek yogurt, cottage cheese, lean turkey or chicken, tofu, and plant-based protein powders.
3. **Healthy Fats**
   o **Why**: Fats take longer to digest, providing a slow and steady release of energy. They also help your body absorb fat-soluble vitamins and promote brain health.
   o **Examples**: Avocados, nuts, seeds, nut butters, chia seeds, and olive oil.
4. **Fiber-Rich Foods**
   o **Why**: Fiber slows the digestion of carbs and keeps you feeling full longer, preventing overeating and mid-morning hunger pangs.
   o **Examples**: Berries, apples, flaxseeds, chia seeds, whole grains, and leafy greens.

Quick and Easy Breakfast Recipes

Here are some simple, nutrient-packed breakfast ideas that will keep you energized and focused all morning long:

Overnight Oats with Chia Seeds

Preparation Time: 5 minutes | **Cooking Time:** None (overnight refrigeration) | **Servings:** 1

- **Ingredients:**

  1. 1/2 cup rolled oats
  2. 1 tablespoon chia seeds
  3. 1/2 cup Greek yogurt
  4. 1/2 cup almond milk (or any milk of choice)
  5. 1/2 cup mixed berries
  6. 1 teaspoon honey or maple syrup (optional)

- **Instructions:**

  1. Combine oats, chia seeds, Greek yogurt, and almond milk in a jar or bowl.

2. Stir in berries and sweetener, if using.
3. Cover and refrigerate overnight.
4. In the morning, give it a stir and enjoy!

- **Nutritional Information:**

Calories: 320 | Carbohydrates: 45g | Protein: 15g | Fat: 10g | Fiber: 12g

Avocado Toast with Poached Egg

Preparation Time: 5 minutes | **Cooking Time:** 5 minutes | **Servings:** 1

- **Ingredients:**

  1. 1 slice whole-grain bread
  2. 1/2 avocado, mashed
  3. 1 poached egg
  4. Salt, pepper, and red pepper flakes (to taste)

- **Instructions:**

  1. Toast the whole-grain bread.
  2. Spread the mashed avocado on the toast and season with salt and pepper.
  3. Top with the poached egg and sprinkle red pepper flakes if desired.

- **Nutritional Information:**

Calories: 280 | Carbohydrates: 22g | Protein: 12g | Fat: 18g | Fiber: 7g

Greek Yogurt Parfait with Nuts and Berries

Preparation Time: 5 minutes | **Cooking Time:** None | **Servings:** 1

- **Ingredients:**

  1. 1 cup Greek yogurt
  2. 1/4 cup mixed nuts (almonds, walnuts, etc.)
  3. 1/2 cup mixed berries (blueberries, raspberries, strawberries)
  4. 1 tablespoon flaxseeds or chia seeds

- **Instructions:**

  1. Layer Greek yogurt, berries, and nuts in a glass or bowl.
  2. Sprinkle with flaxseeds or chia seeds for added fiber and healthy fats.

3. Enjoy immediately or pack in a jar for a quick on-the-go breakfast.

- **Nutritional Information:**

Calories: 350 | Carbohydrates: 30g | Protein: 20g | Fat: 18g | Fiber: 7g

Veggie-Packed Scrambled Eggs

Preparation Time: 5 minutes | **Cooking Time:** 5 minutes | **Servings:** 1

- **Ingredients:**

  1. 2 eggs
  2. 1/2 cup spinach, chopped
  3. 1/4 cup bell peppers, diced
  4. 1/4 cup mushrooms, sliced
  5. 1 tablespoon olive oil
  6. Salt and pepper to taste

- **Instructions:**

  1. Heat olive oil in a skillet over medium heat.
  2. Add the veggies and sauté until softened.
  3. Beat the eggs in a bowl and pour over the veggies.
  4. Scramble until cooked through. Season with salt and pepper and enjoy!

- **Nutritional Information:**

Calories: 220 | Carbohydrates: 6g | Protein: 14g | Fat: 16g | Fiber: 2g

Green Smoothie

Preparation Time: 5 minutes | **Cooking Time:** None | **Servings:** 1

- **Ingredients:**

  1. 1 cup spinach or kale
  2. 1/2 banana
  3. 1/2 cup Greek yogurt
  4. 1 tablespoon almond butter or peanut butter
  5. 1/2 cup unsweetened almond milk (or milk of choice)
  6. 1 tablespoon chia seeds

- **Instructions**:

    1. Blend all ingredients together until smooth.
    2. Pour into a glass and enjoy or take it on the go for a quick breakfast.

- **Nutritional Information:**

Calories: 250 | Carbohydrates: 30g | Protein: 12g | Fat: 10g | Fiber: 8g Information:

Peanut Butter Banana Smoothie

Preparation Time: 5 minutes | **Cooking Time:** None | **Servings:** 1

- **Ingredients:**

    1. 1 banana
    2. 1 tablespoon peanut butter
    3. 1/2 cup Greek yogurt
    4. 1/2 cup almond milk
    5. 1 tablespoon flaxseeds

- **Instructions:**

    1. Blend all ingredients until smooth.
    2. Pour into a glass and enjoy immediately.

- **Nutritional Information:**

Calories: 310 | Carbohydrates: 38g | Protein: 14g | Fat: 13g | Fiber: 6g

Spinach and Feta Omelette

Preparation Time: 5 minutes | **Cooking Time:** 5 minutes | **Servings:** 1

- **Ingredients:**

    1. 2 eggs
    2. 1/4 cup spinach, chopped
    3. 2 tablespoons feta cheese
    4. 1 teaspoon olive oil
    5. Salt and pepper to taste

- **Instructions:**

  1. Heat olive oil in a pan and sauté spinach until wilted.
  2. Beat the eggs, then pour into the pan with spinach.
  3. Add feta cheese and cook until the eggs are fully set.
  4. Season with salt and pepper and serve.

- **Nutritional Information:**

Calories: 240 | Carbohydrates: 2g | Protein: 16g | Fat: 19g | Fiber: 1g

Apple Cinnamon Quinoa Bowl

Preparation Time: 5 minutes | **Cooking Time:** 10 minutes | **Servings:** 1

- **Ingredients:**

  1. 1/2 cup cooked quinoa
  2. 1/2 apple, diced
  3. 1 teaspoon cinnamon
  4. 1 tablespoon walnuts, chopped
  5. 1 teaspoon honey

- **Instructions:**

  1. Mix cooked quinoa with diced apple, cinnamon, and honey.
  2. Top with walnuts and enjoy warm.

- **Nutritional Information:**

Calories: 280 | Carbohydrates: 45g | Protein: 7g | Fat: 8g | Fiber: 6g

Cottage Cheese with Berries and Almonds

Preparation Time: 5 minutes | **Cooking Time:** None | **Servings:** 1

- **Ingredients:**

  1. 1/2 cup cottage cheese
  2. 1/4 cup mixed berries
  3. 1 tablespoon almonds, chopped

- **Instructions:**

    1. Spoon cottage cheese into a bowl and top with berries and almonds.
    2. Serve immediately for a light, refreshing breakfast.

- **Nutritional Information:**

Calories: 200 | Carbohydrates: 14g | Protein: 17g | Fat: 8g | Fiber: 3g

Whole-Grain Waffles with Almond Butter

Preparation Time: 5 minutes | **Cooking Time:** 5 minutes | **Servings:** 1

- **Ingredients:**

    1. 2 whole-grain waffles
    2. 1 tablespoon almond butter
    3. 1 teaspoon chia seeds

- **Instructions:**

    1. Toast the waffles until golden and crispy.
    2. Spread almond butter on top and sprinkle with chia seeds.
    3. Serve immediately.

- **Nutritional Information:**

Calories: 340 | Carbohydrates: 38g | Protein: 11g | Fat: 18g | Fiber: 6g

Tips for a Balanced Breakfast Routine

1. **Meal Prep When You Can**: Preparing ingredients or meals ahead of time—like overnight oats or smoothie packs—can save you time in the morning while ensuring you get a nutritious start to your day.
2. **Mix and Match**: Don't be afraid to experiment with different combinations of proteins, carbs, and fats. For example, swap out the Greek yogurt in your parfait for a plant-based yogurt, or try a different type of nut butter in your smoothie.
3. **Avoid Sugary Breakfast Foods**: Cereals, pastries, and sugary drinks can cause blood sugar spikes, leading to energy crashes shortly after breakfast. Instead, opt for whole grains, fruits, and protein-rich options for a more stable energy source.
4. **Stay Hydrated**: Don't forget to hydrate in the morning. A glass of water or a cup of herbal tea can help kickstart your metabolism and keep your energy levels steady.

Chapter 4: Energizing Lunches

Your midday meal is crucial for maintaining productivity and energy levels throughout the afternoon. A well-balanced lunch provides the nutrients your body needs to power through the rest of the day, preventing the dreaded afternoon slump that can leave you feeling tired, sluggish, and unfocused. By incorporating complex carbohydrates, lean proteins, and healthy fats, you ensure that your body has the sustained fuel it needs to avoid energy crashes and keep you feeling alert and productive.

Fuelling Your Midday for Productivity

When you skip lunch or opt for a meal high in refined sugars and simple carbohydrates, your blood sugar spikes quickly and drops just as fast, leaving you drained and struggling to concentrate. On the other hand, when you prioritize whole foods that digest slowly, you maintain steady energy, helping you stay sharp and focused whether you're working on a project, attending meetings, or simply managing your daily tasks.

The right lunch isn't just about fuelling your body; it's about fuelling your mind as well. A nutrient-rich meal supports mental clarity, decision-making, and creativity, allowing you to stay productive and engaged. By choosing foods that provide lasting energy, you can optimize your performance and avoid the need for mid-afternoon snacks or caffeine pick-me-ups.

Recipes for Power Lunches

Here's a collection of energizing power lunches designed to keep your energy levels high, help you stay focused, and prevent those post-lunch energy crashes:

Quinoa & Avocado Power Bowl

Preparation Time: 10 minutes | **Cooking Time:** 15 minutes | **Servings:** 1

- **Ingredients**:

    1. 1/2 cup cooked quinoa
    2. 1/4 avocado, sliced
    3. 1/2 cup cherry tomatoes, halved
    4. 1/4 cup cucumber, diced
    5. 1 tablespoon olive oil
    6. 1 tablespoon lemon juice
    7. Salt and pepper to taste

- **Instructions**:

  1. Combine the cooked quinoa, cherry tomatoes, cucumber, and avocado in a bowl.
  2. Drizzle with olive oil and lemon juice, then season with salt and pepper. Toss gently to combine.
  3. Serve immediately for a refreshing and energizing lunch.

- **Nutritional Information:**

Calories: 350 | Carbohydrates: 38g | Protein: 8g | Fat: 20g | Fiber: 8g

Grilled Chicken & Veggie Wrap

Preparation Time: 10 minutes | **Cooking Time:** 15 minutes | **Servings:** 1

- **Ingredients**:

  1. 1 whole-wheat wrap
  2. 3 oz grilled chicken breast, sliced
  3. 1/4 cup spinach leaves
  4. 1/4 cup bell peppers, sliced
  5. 1 tablespoon hummus
  6. 1 tablespoon Greek yogurt

- **Instructions**:

  1. Spread hummus and Greek yogurt onto the whole-wheat wrap.
  2. Layer grilled chicken, spinach, and bell peppers.
  3. Roll the wrap tightly and serve.

- **Nutritional Information:**

Calories: 320 | Carbohydrates: 28g | Protein: 28g | Fat: 10g | Fiber: 5g

Lentil & Sweet Potato Salad

Preparation Time: 10 minutes | **Cooking Time:** 25 minutes | **Servings:** 2

- **Ingredients**:

  1. 1/2 cup cooked lentils
  2. 1 small, sweet potato, diced
  3. 1/4 cup red onion, finely chopped
  4. 2 tablespoons olive oil
  5. 1 tablespoon balsamic vinegar

6. Salt and pepper to taste

- **Instructions**:

1. Roast the sweet potato in the oven at 400°F (200°C) for 25 minutes or until tender.
2. Combine the cooked lentils, roasted sweet potato, and red onion in a bowl.
3. Drizzle with olive oil and balsamic vinegar. Toss to combine and season with salt and pepper.

- **Nutritional Information**:

Calories: 400 | Carbohydrates: 55g | Protein: 14g | Fat: 12g | Fiber: 12g

Turkey and Spinach Quinoa Salad

Preparation Time: 10 minutes | **Cooking Time:** 20 minutes | **Servings:** 2

- **Ingredients**:

1. 1/2 cup cooked quinoa
2. 1 cup spinach, chopped
3. 3 oz cooked turkey breast, sliced
4. 1 tablespoon olive oil
5. 1 tablespoon lemon juice
6. 1 tablespoon sunflower seeds

- **Instructions**:

1. In a large bowl, combine the cooked quinoa, spinach, and turkey breast.
2. Drizzle with olive oil and lemon juice, and top with sunflower seeds.
3. Toss well and serve.

- **Nutritional Information**:

Calories: 360 | Carbohydrates: 34g | Protein: 28g | Fat: 14g | Fiber: 6g

Chickpea Salad with Cucumber & Tomatoes

Preparation Time: 10 minutes | **Cooking Time:** None | **Servings:** 1

- **Ingredients**:

1. 1/2 cup canned chickpeas, drained and rinsed
2. 1/4 cup cucumber, diced
3. 1/4 cup cherry tomatoes, halved

4. 1 tablespoon olive oil
5. 1 tablespoon lemon juice
6. Salt and pepper to taste

- **Instructions**:

1. In a bowl, combine chickpeas, cucumber, and tomatoes.
2. Drizzle with olive oil and lemon juice, then season with salt and pepper.
3. Toss gently and serve.

- **Nutritional Information**:

Calories: 260 | Carbohydrates: 32g | Protein: 8g | Fat: 12g | Fiber: 8g

Tuna Salad with Mixed Greens

Preparation Time: 10 minutes | **Cooking Time:** None | **Servings:** 1

- **Ingredients**:

1. 1 can tuna in water, drained
2. 2 cups mixed greens (spinach, arugula, lettuce)
3. 1/4 cup cucumber, sliced
4. 1 tablespoon olive oil
5. 1 tablespoon balsamic vinegar
6. Salt and pepper to taste

- **Instructions**:

1. Place the mixed greens, cucumber, and tuna in a bowl.
2. Drizzle with olive oil and balsamic vinegar.
3. Toss gently and serve.

- **Nutritional Information**:

Calories: 220 | Carbohydrates: 6g | Protein: 32g | Fat: 10g | Fiber: 3g

Grilled Salmon & Asparagus

Preparation Time: 10 minutes | **Cooking Time:** 15 minutes | **Servings:** 1

- **Ingredients:**

  1. 4 oz grilled salmon
  2. 1/2 bunch asparagus, trimmed
  3. 1 tablespoon olive oil
  4. 1 tablespoon lemon juice
  5. Salt and pepper to taste

- **Instructions:**

  1. Grill the salmon until fully cooked, about 10-12 minutes.
  2. Toss the asparagus with olive oil, salt, and pepper, then grill for 5-7 minutes.
  3. Serve the salmon and asparagus together, drizzled with lemon juice.

- **Nutritional Information:**

  Calories: 350 | Carbohydrates: 8g | Protein: 28g | Fat: 24g | Fiber: 4g

Black Bean & Quinoa Stir-Fry

Preparation Time: 10 minutes | **Cooking Time:** 15 minutes | **Servings:** 2

- **Ingredients:**

  1. 1/2 cup cooked quinoa
  2. 1/2 cup black beans, rinsed
  3. 1/2 cup bell peppers, sliced
  4. 1 tablespoon olive oil
  5. 1 tablespoon soy sauce

- **Instructions:**

  1. In a skillet, heat olive oil and sauté the bell peppers until soft.
  2. Add the black beans, cooked quinoa, and soy sauce. Stir and cook for 5 minutes.
  3. Serve hot.

- **Nutritional Information:**

  Calories: 320 | Carbohydrates: 48g | Protein: 12g | Fat: 10g | Fiber: 10g

Eggplant & Zucchini Wrap

Preparation Time: 10 minutes | **Cooking Time:** 15 minutes | **Servings:** 1

- **Ingredients:**

  1. 1 whole-wheat wrap
  2. 1/2 cup grilled eggplant, sliced
  3. 1/2 cup grilled zucchini, sliced
  4. 1 tablespoon hummus
  5. 1 tablespoon feta cheese

- **Instructions:**

  1. Spread hummus on the whole-wheat wrap.
  2. Add grilled eggplant, zucchini, and feta cheese.
  3. Roll the wrap and serve.

- **Nutritional Information:**

  Calories: 300 | Carbohydrates: 40g | Protein: 10g | Fat: 12g | Fiber: 8g

Tofu & Broccoli Stir-Fry

Preparation Time: 10 minutes | **Cooking Time:** 15 minutes | **Servings:** 2

- **Ingredients:**

  1. 1/2 block tofu, cubed
  2. 1 cup broccoli florets
  3. 1 tablespoon olive oil
  4. 1 tablespoon soy sauce
  5. 1 tablespoon sesame seeds

- **Instructions:**

  1. Heat olive oil in a pan and sauté the tofu cubes until golden.
  2. Add broccoli and cook for 5-7 minutes.
  3. Drizzle with soy sauce and sprinkle with sesame seeds. Serve hot.

- **Nutritional Information:**

  Calories: 320 | Carbohydrates: 18g | Protein: 20g | Fat: 18g | Fiber: 6g

Chapter 5: Dinner for Recovery and Relaxation

Dinner isn't just about ending your day with a satisfying meal; it plays a vital role in helping your body recover and prepare for the next day. After a long day of activities—whether it's work, exercise, or taking care of family—your body needs the right nutrients to recover, repair, and restore. An ideal dinner provides a balance of lean protein, healthy fats, and fiber-rich vegetables to support muscle recovery, promote restful sleep, and keep energy levels balanced through the evening.

Why Dinner Matters for Recovery and Relaxation

By the time dinner rolls around, your body has worked hard all day, using energy and resources to keep you moving and thinking clearly. A well-balanced dinner helps your body:

- **Repair Muscles**: Lean proteins support muscle repair and growth, which is especially important if you've been physically active.
- **Promote Restful Sleep**: Healthy fats and complex carbohydrates play a role in regulating hormones like serotonin and melatonin, which promote relaxation and improve sleep quality.
- **Prevent Late-Night Hunger**: Fiber-rich foods and balanced meals prevent hunger pangs late at night, keeping you full and satisfied until morning.
- **Support Overall Recovery**: A combination of vitamins, minerals, and antioxidants from vegetables and whole foods helps fight inflammation and supports your body's natural recovery processes.

Energizing Dinner Recipes

Here are 10 nutrient-dense, easy-to-prepare dinners designed to help your body recover, relax, and get ready for a restful night.

Baked Salmon with Roasted Vegetables

Preparation Time: 10 minutes | **Cooking Time:** 25 minutes | **Servings:** 1

- **Ingredients**:

  1. 4 oz salmon fillet
  2. 1/2 cup broccoli florets
  3. 1/2 cup sweet potatoes, diced
  4. 1 tablespoon olive oil
  5. 1 tablespoon lemon juice
  6. Salt and pepper to taste

- **Instructions**:

  1. Preheat the oven to 400°F (200°C).

2. Toss the sweet potatoes and broccoli in olive oil, then roast for 25 minutes.
3. While vegetables roast, season the salmon with lemon juice, salt, and pepper.
4. Bake the salmon for 12-15 minutes or until fully cooked.
5. Serve the salmon with roasted vegetables.

- **Nutritional Information:**

Calories: 400 | Carbohydrates: 28g | Protein: 35g | Fat: 18g | Fiber: 6g

Chicken Stir-Fry with Brown Rice

Preparation Time: 10 minutes | **Cooking Time:** 15 minutes | **Servings:** 1

- **Ingredients:**

1. 4 oz chicken breast, sliced
2. 1/2 cup brown rice, cooked
3. 1/2 cup bell peppers, sliced
4. 1/4 cup broccoli florets
5. 1 tablespoon olive oil
6. 1 tablespoon soy sauce

- **Instructions:**

1. Heat olive oil in a pan and stir-fry the chicken until fully cooked.
2. Add the bell peppers and broccoli, sauté for 3-5 minutes.
3. Stir in soy sauce and serve over cooked brown rice.

- **Nutritional Information:**

Calories: 350 | Carbohydrates: 38g | Protein: 30g | Fat: 10g | Fiber: 5g

Quinoa-Stuffed Bell Peppers

Preparation Time: 10 minutes | **Cooking Time:** 30 minutes | **Servings:** 2

- **Ingredients:**

1. 2 bell peppers, tops removed and seeded
2. 1/2 cup cooked quinoa
3. 1/4 cup black beans
4. 1/4 cup corn
5. 1 tablespoon olive oil
6. 1 tablespoon salsa

- **Instructions**:

  1. Preheat the oven to 375°F (190°C).
  2. Mix quinoa, black beans, corn, olive oil, and salsa.
  3. Stuff the mixture into the bell peppers and bake for 30 minutes.

- **Nutritional Information:**

Calories: 320 | Carbohydrates: 50g | Protein: 12g | Fat: 10g | Fiber: 8g

Turkey Meatballs with Zucchini Noodles

Preparation Time: 10 minutes | **Cooking Time:** 20 minutes | **Servings:** 2

- **Ingredients**:

  1. 4 oz ground turkey
  2. 1/2 cup zucchini noodles
  3. 1 tablespoon olive oil
  4. 1/2 cup marinara sauce

- **Instructions**:

  1. Roll the ground turkey into small meatballs and cook in olive oil until browned.
  2. Add marinara sauce and simmer for 10 minutes.
  3. Serve over zucchini noodles.

- **Nutritional Information:**

Calories: 350 | Carbohydrates: 12g | Protein: 28g | Fat: 20g | Fiber: 4g

Tofu Stir-Fry with Vegetables

Preparation Time: 10 minutes | **Cooking Time:** 15 minutes | **Servings:** 2

- **Ingredients**:

  1. 1/2 block tofu, cubed
  2. 1/2 cup carrots, sliced
  3. 1/2 cup broccoli florets
  4. 1 tablespoon olive oil
  5. 1 tablespoon soy sauce

- Instructions:

  1. Heat olive oil in a pan and stir-fry tofu until golden.
  2. Add carrots, broccoli, and soy sauce; sauté for 5-7 minutes.
  3. Serve hot.

- Nutritional Information:

Calories: 300 | Carbohydrates: 20g | Protein: 18g | Fat: 18g | Fiber: 6g

Grilled Chicken with Avocado Salsa

Preparation Time: 10 minutes | **Cooking Time:** 15 minutes | **Servings:** 1

- Ingredients:

  1. 4 oz grilled chicken breast
  2. 1/4 avocado, diced
  3. 1/4 cup cherry tomatoes, diced
  4. 1 tablespoon lime juice
  5. Salt and pepper to taste

- Instructions:

  1. Grill chicken until fully cooked.
  2. Combine avocado, tomatoes, and lime juice to make salsa.
  3. Top chicken with avocado salsa and serve.

- Nutritional Information:

Calories: 320 | Carbohydrates: 10g | Protein: 35g | Fat: 18g | Fiber: 5g

Baked Cod with Spinach

Preparation Time: 10 minutes | **Cooking Time:** 20 minutes | **Servings:** 1

- Ingredients:

  1. 4 oz cod fillet
  2. 1 cup spinach, sautéed
  3. 1 tablespoon olive oil
  4. 1 tablespoon lemon juice
  5. Salt and pepper to taste

- **Instructions**:

    1. Preheat the oven to 375°F (190°C).
    2. Season cod with olive oil, lemon juice, salt, and pepper. Bake for 20 minutes.
    3. Serve with sautéed spinach.

- **Nutritional Information:**

Calories: 280 | Carbohydrates: 5g | Protein: 32g | Fat: 15g | Fiber: 3g

Lemon Garlic Baked Cod with Steamed Broccoli

Preparation Time: 10 minutes | **Cooking Time:** 15 minutes | **Servings:** 2

- **Ingredients**:

    1. 2 cod fillets (4-6 oz each)
    2. 1 tablespoon olive oil
    3. 1 tablespoon lemon juice
    4. 2 garlic cloves, minced
    5. 1 teaspoon dried oregano
    6. Salt and pepper to taste
    7. 1 small head of broccoli, cut into florets
    8. 1 tablespoon fresh parsley, chopped (optional for garnish)

- **Instructions**:

    1. Preheat the oven to 375°F (190°C).
    2. In a small bowl, mix olive oil, lemon juice, minced garlic, oregano, salt, and pepper.
    3. Place the cod fillets on a baking sheet lined with parchment paper. Drizzle the lemon garlic mixture over the fillets.
    4. Bake the cod for 12-15 minutes, or until it flakes easily with a fork.
    5. While the cod is baking, steam the broccoli florets for about 5 minutes until tender but still crisp.
    6. Serve the baked cod with steamed broccoli, and garnish with fresh parsley if desired.

- **Nutritional Information (per serving):**

Calories: 250 | Carbohydrates: 8g | Protein: 30g | Fat: 10g | Fiber: 4g

Shrimp Stir-Fry with Bok Choy

Preparation Time: 10 minutes | **Cooking Time:** 10 minutes | **Servings:** 1

- **Ingredients**:

    1. 4 oz shrimp, peeled and deveined
    2. 1 cup bok choy, chopped
    3. 1 tablespoon olive oil
    4. 1 tablespoon soy sauce

- **Instructions**:

    1. Heat olive oil in a pan and stir-fry shrimp until pink.
    2. Add bok choy and soy sauce, cooking for 3-5 minutes.
    3. Serve immediately.

- **Nutritional Information:**

Calories: 280 | Carbohydrates: 6g | Protein: 30g | Fat: 14g | Fiber: 4g

Beef & Broccoli Stir-Fry

Preparation Time: 10 minutes | **Cooking Time:** 15 minutes | **Servings:** 2

- **Ingredients**:

    1. 4 oz lean beef strips
    2. 1/2 cup broccoli florets
    3. 1 tablespoon olive oil
    4. 1 tablespoon soy sauce

- **Instructions**:

    1. Heat olive oil in a pan and stir-fry beef strips until cooked.
    2. Add broccoli and soy sauce, sauté for 5-7 minutes.
    3. Serve hot.

- **Nutritional Information:**

Calories: 380 | Carbohydrates: 10g | Protein: 30g | Fat: 24g | Fiber: 4g

Chapter 6: Snacks to Keep You Going

Snacking isn't just a way to satisfy hunger between meals—it's an opportunity to keep your energy levels steady, your mind sharp, and your body fuelled. The right snacks can help you avoid the common energy dips that often occur in the afternoon or between meals. Instead of reaching for sugary or processed snacks that lead to quick energy crashes, you can choose nutrient-dense options that provide long-lasting fuel.

Why Snacks Matter for Energy

When your body goes too long without food, blood sugar levels can drop, leading to fatigue, brain fog, irritability, and cravings for unhealthy foods. Snacking on the right foods helps stabilize your blood sugar levels, giving you a steady stream of energy while also preventing overeating at your next meal.

Balanced snacks that include a mix of protein, fiber, and healthy fats ensure a slower digestion process, providing you with long-lasting energy rather than quick spikes and crashes. These types of snacks also promote mental clarity and focus, helping you stay productive throughout the day.

Energizing Snack Recipes

Here are 10 easy-to-make, energizing snack options that will keep you fuelled between meals and prevent energy crashes.

Roasted Chickpeas

Preparation Time: 5 minutes | **Cooking Time:** 25 minutes | **Servings:** 2

- **Ingredients:**

  1. 1 can chickpeas, drained and rinsed
  2. 1 tablespoon olive oil
  3. 1 teaspoon paprika
  4. Salt and pepper to taste

- **Instructions:**

  1. Preheat oven to 400°F (200°C).
  2. Toss chickpeas with olive oil, paprika, salt, and pepper.

3. Spread on a baking sheet and roast for 25 minutes until crispy.
4. Enjoy as a crunchy, protein-packed snack.

- **Nutritional Information:**

Calories: 180 | Carbohydrates: 28g | Protein: 8g | Fat: 6g | Fiber: 6g

Apple Slices with Almond Butter

Preparation Time: 5 minutes | **Cooking Time:** None | **Servings:** 1

- **Ingredients:**

  1. 1 apple, sliced
  2. 1 tablespoon almond butter

- **Instructions:**

  1. Slice the apple and spread almond butter on each slice.
  2. Enjoy immediately for a refreshing, fiber-rich snack.

- **Nutritional Information:**

Calories: 190 | Carbohydrates: 25g | Protein: 4g | Fat: 9g | Fiber: 5g

Greek Yogurt with Honey and Walnuts

Preparation Time: 5 minutes | **Cooking Time:** None | **Servings:** 1

- **Ingredients:**

  1. 1/2 cup Greek yogurt
  2. 1 tablespoon honey
  3. 1 tablespoon walnuts, chopped

- **Instructions:**

  1. Spoon the Greek yogurt into a bowl.
  2. Drizzle with honey and top with walnuts.
  3. Enjoy this protein-packed and omega-3-rich snack.

- **Nutritional Information:**

Calories: 220 | Carbohydrates: 22g | Protein: 10g | Fat: 10g | Fiber: 2g

Hummus with Veggie Sticks

Preparation Time: 5 minutes | **Cooking Time:** None | **Servings:** 1

- **Ingredients**:

  1. 1/4 cup hummus
  2. 1/2 cup carrot sticks
  3. 1/2 cup cucumber sticks

- **Instructions**:

  1. Serve hummus with carrot and cucumber sticks for dipping.
  2. Enjoy as a refreshing, fiber-rich snack.

- **Nutritional Information:**

  Calories: 180 | Carbohydrates: 22g | Protein: 4g | Fat: 8g | Fiber: 6g

Hard-Boiled Eggs with Avocado

Preparation Time: 5 minutes | **Cooking Time:** 10 minutes | **Servings:** 1

- **Ingredients**:

  1. 2 hard-boiled eggs
  2. 1/4 avocado, sliced
  3. Salt and pepper to taste

- **Instructions**:

  1. Slice the hard-boiled eggs and top with avocado slices.
  2. Season with salt and pepper for a protein-rich, healthy-fat snack.

- **Nutritional Information:**

  Calories: 240 | Carbohydrates: 4g | Protein: 12g | Fat: 18g | Fiber: 3g

Energy Balls with Oats and Peanut Butter

Preparation Time: 10 minutes | **Cooking Time:** None | **Servings:** 10 balls

- **Ingredients:**

  1. 1 cup rolled oats
  2. 1/2 cup peanut butter
  3. 1/4 cup honey
  4. 1/4 cup flaxseeds

- **Instructions:**

  1. Combine all ingredients in a bowl.
  2. Roll into small balls and refrigerate for 20 minutes.
  3. Enjoy these energy-packed bites whenever you need a quick boost.

- **Nutritional Information (per ball):**

  Calories: 110 | Carbohydrates: 10g | Protein: 4g | Fat: 7g | Fiber: 2g

Cottage Cheese with Pineapple

Preparation Time: 5 minutes | **Cooking Time:** None | **Servings:** 1

- **Ingredients:**

  1. 1/2 cup cottage cheese
  2. 1/4 cup pineapple, diced

- **Instructions:**

  1. Combine the cottage cheese and pineapple in a bowl.
  2. Serve as a light, protein-rich snack with a touch of natural sweetness.

- **Nutritional Information:**

  Calories: 150 | Carbohydrates: 12g | Protein: 12g | Fat: 5g | Fiber: 1g

Whole-Grain Crackers with Tuna Salad

Preparation Time: 10 minutes | **Cooking Time:** None | **Servings:** 1

- **Ingredients:**

  1. 1 can tuna in water, drained
  2. 1 tablespoon Greek yogurt
  3. 6 whole-grain crackers

- **Instructions:**
  1. Mix tuna with Greek yogurt.
  2. Serve with whole-grain crackers for a satisfying and protein-packed snack.

- **Nutritional Information:**

  Calories: 220 | Carbohydrates: 18g | Protein: 22g | Fat: 7g | Fiber: 4g

Chia Pudding with Berries

Preparation Time: 5 minutes | **Cooking Time:** None | **Servings:** 1

- **Ingredients:**

  1. 2 tablespoons chia seeds
  2. 1/2 cup almond milk
  3. 1/4 cup mixed berries

- **Instructions:**

  1. Mix chia seeds with almond milk and let sit for at least 20 minutes (or overnight).
  2. Top with berries and enjoy this high-fiber, omega-3-rich snack.

- **Nutritional Information:**

  Calories: 170 | Carbohydrates: 18g | Protein: 5g | Fat: 9g | Fiber: 8g

Almonds with Dark Chocolate

Preparation Time: 2 minutes | **Cooking Time:** None | **Servings:** 1

- **Ingredients:**

  1. 10 almonds
  2. 1 oz dark chocolate (70% cacao or higher)

- **Instructions:**

  1. Enjoy almonds with a piece of dark chocolate for a satisfying combination of healthy fats and antioxidants.

- **Nutritional Information:**

Calories: 220 | Carbohydrates: 16g | Protein: 5g | Fat: 14g | Fiber: 5g

Chapter 7: Healthy Desserts for Sweet Energy

Who says dessert can't be healthy and energizing? The key to enjoying sweets without the guilt (or the energy crash) is to choose desserts made from nutrient-dense ingredients that provide slow-releasing energy. When made with the right balance of healthy fats, natural sweeteners, and fiber-rich ingredients, desserts can not only satisfy your sweet tooth but also fuel your body with lasting energy.

Why Healthy Desserts Matter for Energy

Traditional desserts often rely on refined sugars and unhealthy fats that provide a quick burst of energy followed by a sharp crash. These energy spikes can leave you feeling tired and craving more sugar. Instead, healthy desserts are crafted with whole foods that provide nutrients your body can use for longer-lasting energy. Ingredients like **natural sweeteners**, **fiber-rich fruits**, and **healthy fats** keep blood sugar levels stable and prevent those sugar highs and lows.

Healthy desserts also include ingredients that provide additional benefits beyond energy, such as **antioxidants**, **fiber**, and **essential vitamins** that support overall well-being. So, you can enjoy a sweet treat while nourishing your body at the same time.

Energizing Dessert Recipes

Here are 10 delicious and healthy dessert recipes that will satisfy your sweet tooth while providing your body with lasting energy and nutrition.

<u>Dark Chocolate Almond Bites</u>

Preparation Time: 10 minutes | **Cooking Time:** None | **Servings:** 12 bites

- **Ingredients**:

  1. 1/2 cup dark chocolate (70% cacao or higher), melted
  2. 1/4 cup almonds, chopped
  3. 1 tablespoon coconut oil

- **Instructions**:

    1. Mix melted dark chocolate and coconut oil.
    2. Stir in chopped almonds and pour into a silicone mold or lined tray.
    3. Refrigerate for 30 minutes until firm.
    4. Enjoy these antioxidant-rich, healthy fat bites.

- **Nutritional Information (per bite):**

Calories: 80 | Carbohydrates: 5g | Protein: 1g | Fat: 6g | Fiber: 1g

Chia Pudding with Coconut and Berries

Preparation Time: 5 minutes | **Cooking Time:** None (refrigerate overnight) | **Servings:** 1

- **Ingredients**:

    1. 1/4 cup chia seeds
    2. 1 cup unsweetened coconut milk
    3. 1 tablespoon honey or maple syrup
    4. 1/4 cup mixed berries

- **Instructions**:

    1. Combine chia seeds, coconut milk, and honey in a bowl. Stir well.
    2. Refrigerate overnight to allow the chia seeds to absorb the liquid.
    3. Top with fresh berries before serving.

- **Nutritional Information (per bite):**

Calories: 220 | Carbohydrates: 30g | Protein: 6g | Fat: 9g | Fiber: 10g

Banana Oat Cookies

Preparation Time: 5 minutes | **Cooking Time:** 15 minutes | **Servings:** 12 cookies

- **Ingredients**:

    1. 2 ripe bananas, mashed
    2. 1 cup rolled oats
    3. 1/4 cup almond butter
    4. 1/4 cup dark chocolate chips

- **Instructions:**

  1. Preheat oven to 350°F (175°C).
  2. Mix mashed bananas, oats, almond butter, and chocolate chips.
  3. Drop spoonfuls of the mixture onto a baking sheet and bake for 12-15 minutes.
  4. Let cool and enjoy.

- **Nutritional Information (per cookie):**

Calories: 90 | Carbohydrates: 12g | Protein: 2g | Fat: 4g | Fiber: 2g

Greek Yogurt Bark with Berries

Preparation Time: 5 minutes | **Cooking Time:** None (freeze for 2 hours) | **Servings:** 1

- **Ingredients:**

  1. 1 cup Greek yogurt
  2. 1 tablespoon honey
  3. 1/4 cup mixed berries
  4. 1 tablespoon chia seeds

- **Instructions:**

  1. Spread Greek yogurt on a parchment-lined baking sheet.
  2. Top with berries, chia seeds, and honey.
  3. Freeze for at least 2 hours until firm. Break into pieces and enjoy.

- **Nutritional Information (per cookie):**

Calories: 150 | Carbohydrates: 22g | Protein: 10g | Fat: 3g | Fiber: 3g

Sweet Potato Brownies

Preparation Time: 10 minutes | **Cooking Time:** 25 minutes | **Servings:** 12 brownies

- **Ingredients:**

  1. 1 cup mashed sweet potato
  2. 1/2 cup almond flour
  3. 1/4 cup cocoa powder
  4. 1/4 cup maple syrup

- **Instructions**:

    1. Preheat oven to 350°F (175°C).
    2. Mix sweet potato, almond flour, cocoa powder, and maple syrup.
    3. Pour into a lined baking dish and bake for 25 minutes.
    4. Let cool and cut into squares.

- **Nutritional Information (per brownie):**

Calories: 120 | Carbohydrates: 18g | Protein: 3g | Fat: 5g | Fiber: 3g

Avocado Chocolate Mousse

Preparation Time: 5 minutes | **Cooking Time:** None | **Servings:** 2

- **Ingredients**:

    1. 1 ripe avocado
    2. 2 tablespoons cocoa powder
    3. 2 tablespoons honey or maple syrup
    4. 1/4 cup almond milk

- **Instructions**:

    1. Blend all ingredients until smooth.
    2. Chill in the fridge for 10 minutes before serving.

- **Nutritional Information:**

Calories: 220 | Carbohydrates: 25g | Protein: 4g | Fat: 14g | Fiber: 6g

Peanut Butter Date Energy Balls

Preparation Time: 10 minutes | **Cooking Time:** None | **Servings:** 12 balls

- **Ingredients:**

  1. 1 cup pitted dates
  2. 1/4 cup peanut butter
  3. 1/4 cup oats
  4. 1 tablespoon chia seeds

- **Instructions:**

  1. Blend all ingredients in a food processor.
  2. Roll into small balls and refrigerate for 30 minutes.

- **Nutritional Information (per ball):**

Calories: 90 | Carbohydrates: 12g | Protein: 2g | Fat: 4g | Fiber: 3g

Coconut Macaroons

Preparation Time: 10 minutes | **Cooking Time:** 20 minutes | **Servings:** 12 macaroons

- **Ingredients:**

  1. 1 cup shredded coconut
  2. 2 egg whites
  3. 1/4 cup honey
  4. 1 teaspoon vanilla extract

- **Instructions:**

  1. Preheat oven to 350°F (175°C).
  2. Mix coconut, egg whites, honey, and vanilla.
  3. Drop spoonfuls onto a baking sheet and bake for 15-20 minutes.

- **Nutritional Information (per macaroon):**

Calories: 80 | Carbohydrates: 10g | Protein: 2g | Fat: 4g | Fiber: 2g

Oatmeal Raisin Energy Bars

Preparation Time: 10 minutes | **Cooking Time:** 15 minutes | **Servings:** 8 bars

- Ingredients:

  1. 1 cup rolled oats
  2. 1/4 cup raisins
  3. 1/4 cup almond butter
  4. 1/4 cup honey

- Instructions:

  1. Preheat oven to 350°F (175°C).
  2. Mix oats, raisins, almond butter, and honey.
  3. Press into a baking dish and bake for 15 minutes.
  4. Let cool and cut into bars.

- Nutritional Information (per bar):

Calories: 140 | Carbohydrates: 22g | Protein: 4g | Fat: 5g | Fiber: 3g

Frozen Banana Bites with Dark Chocolate

Preparation Time: 5 minutes | **Cooking Time:** None (freeze for 1 hour) | **Servings:** 8 bites

- Ingredients:

  1. 2 bananas, sliced
  2. 1/2 cup dark chocolate (70% cacao or higher), melted
  3. 1 tablespoon peanut butter

- Instructions:

  1. Dip banana slices in melted chocolate and top with a small amount of peanut butter.
  2. Freeze for 1 hour before serving.

- Nutritional Information (per bite):

Calories: 100 | Carbohydrates: 15g | Protein: 2g | Fat: 4g | Fiber: 2g

Chapter 8: Special Diets

Eating for sustained energy is about finding the right balance of nutrients that work for your body, and sometimes, that involves tailoring your diet to meet specific needs. Whether you're following a vegetarian, vegan, gluten-free, low-carb, or other special diet, it's important to ensure that your meals are still packed with the nutrients needed for optimal energy and well-being.

In this chapter, we'll explore different types of special diets, the key nutrients to focus on, and provide tips and recipes to help you stay energized and nourished while adhering to your chosen eating plan.

Why Special Diets Matter for Energy

Different people have different dietary needs, and a special diet can be a way to address health concerns, lifestyle choices, or specific fitness goals. Whether you're eliminating certain foods due to allergies or sensitivities, choosing plant-based options for ethical reasons, or reducing carbohydrates to support weight management, a well-planned special diet can support steady energy levels and overall health.

The key to success with any special diet is ensuring that it remains balanced. Even with food restrictions, it's possible to get all the essential macronutrients (carbohydrates, proteins, fats) and micronutrients (vitamins and minerals) that your body needs to maintain stable energy throughout the day.

Vegetarian Diet

A **vegetarian diet** excludes meat, but it can still be incredibly rich in the nutrients needed for energy. When following a vegetarian diet, it's important to focus on plant-based protein sources and whole grains to keep energy levels high.

Key Nutrients to Focus On:

- **Protein**: Look to beans, lentils, tofu, tempeh, eggs, and dairy for protein sources.
- **Iron**: Leafy greens like spinach, lentils, and fortified cereals are rich in plant-based iron.
- **Vitamin B12**: Since B12 is primarily found in animal products, consider fortified foods or supplements.

Recipes

Lentil and Spinach Salad

Preparation Time: 10 minutes | **Cooking Time:** None | **Servings:** 1

- **Ingredients**:

  1. 1/2 cup cooked lentils
  2. 1 cup spinach, chopped
  3. 1/4 avocado, sliced
  4. 1 tablespoon olive oil
  5. 1 tablespoon lemon juice

- **Instructions**:

  1. Toss the cooked lentils, spinach, and avocado in a bowl.
  2. Drizzle with olive oil and lemon juice, toss to combine, and serve.

- **Nutritional Information**:

Calories: 300 | Carbohydrates: 28g | Protein: 12g | Fat: 16g | Fiber: 10g

Chickpea and Spinach Stir-Fry

Preparation Time: 10 minutes | **Cooking Time:** 10 minutes | **Servings:** 1

- **Ingredients**:

  1. 1/2 cup canned chickpeas, drained and rinsed
  2. 1 cup spinach, chopped
  3. 1/4 cup red bell pepper, diced
  4. 1 tablespoon olive oil
  5. 1 tablespoon soy sauce
  6. 1/2 teaspoon paprika

- **Instructions**:

  1. Heat olive oil in a pan and sauté red bell pepper for 3 minutes.
  2. Add spinach and chickpeas, stir in soy sauce and paprika, and cook for another 5-7 minutes until spinach wilts.
  3. Serve hot.

- **Nutritional Information:**

Calories: 280 | Carbohydrates: 34g | Protein: 10g | Fat: 12g | Fiber: 9g

Sweet Potato and Black Bean Tacos

Preparation Time: 10 minutes | **Cooking Time:** 20 minutes | **Servings:** 2

- **Ingredients:**

  1. 1 medium sweet potato, diced
  2. 1/2 cup black beans, rinsed
  3. 4 small corn tortillas
  4. 1/4 cup red onion, diced
  5. 1 tablespoon olive oil
  6. 1 teaspoon cumin
  7. 1 tablespoon lime juice

- **Instructions:**

  1. Roast the diced sweet potatoes with olive oil and cumin in the oven at 400°F (200°C) for 20 minutes until tender.
  2. Warm the tortillas, then fill each with sweet potatoes, black beans, and diced onion.
  3. Drizzle with lime juice and serve.

- **Nutritional Information (per serving):**

  Calories: 320 | Carbohydrates: 52g | Protein: 10g | Fat: 8g | Fiber: 12g

Lentil and Vegetable Soup

Preparation Time: 10 minutes | **Cooking Time:** 25 minutes | **Servings:** 2

- **Ingredients:**

  1. 1/2 cup dried lentils
  2. 1 carrot, diced
  3. 1 celery stalk, diced
  4. 1/4 cup onion, chopped
  5. 2 cups vegetable broth
  6. 1 tablespoon olive oil
  7. 1 teaspoon cumin

- **Instructions:**
  1. Heat olive oil in a pot and sauté the onion, carrot, and celery until soft.
  2. Add lentils, vegetable broth, and cumin. Bring to a boil, then reduce heat and simmer for 20 minutes until lentils are tender.
  3. Serve hot.

- Nutritional Information (per serving):

Calories: 240 | Carbohydrates: 38g | Protein: 12g | Fat: 7g | Fiber: 10g

Grilled Portobello Mushrooms with Quinoa

Preparation Time: 10 minutes | **Cooking Time:** 20 minutes | **Servings:** 1

- Ingredients:

  1. 2 large portobello mushrooms
  2. 1/2 cup cooked quinoa
  3. 1 tablespoon balsamic vinegar
  4. 1 tablespoon olive oil
  5. Salt and pepper to taste

- Instructions:

  1. Brush portobello mushrooms with balsamic vinegar, olive oil, salt, and pepper. Grill or roast for 15 minutes until tender.
  2. Serve mushrooms on top of cooked quinoa.

- Nutritional Information:

Calories: 280 | Carbohydrates: 35g | Protein: 10g | Fat: 12g | Fiber: 7g

Zucchini Noodles with Pesto

Preparation Time: 10 minutes | **Cooking Time:** 5 minutes | **Servings:** 1

- Ingredients:

  1. 1 medium zucchini, spiralized
  2. 2 tablespoons pesto
  3. 1 tablespoon olive oil
  4. 1 tablespoon Parmesan cheese (optional)

- Instructions:

  1. Heat olive oil in a pan and sauté the zucchini noodles for 2-3 minutes until tender.
  2. Stir in pesto and cook for another 2 minutes.
  3. Top with Parmesan cheese (optional) and serve.

- **Nutritional Information**:

Calories: 250 | Carbohydrates: 10g | Protein: 5g | Fat: 22g | Fiber: 4g

Cauliflower Fried Rice

Preparation Time: 10 minutes | **Cooking Time:** 10 minutes | **Servings:** 1

- **Ingredients**:

  1. 1 cup cauliflower rice
  2. 1/4 cup carrots, diced
  3. 1/4 cup peas
  4. 1 tablespoon soy sauce
  5. 1 tablespoon olive oil
  6. 1/4 teaspoon ginger, minced

- **Instructions**:

  1. Heat olive oil in a pan and sauté carrots and ginger for 3-5 minutes.
  2. Add cauliflower rice and peas and cook for another 5 minutes.
  3. Stir in soy sauce and serve.

- **Nutritional Information**:

Calories: 180 | Carbohydrates: 20g | Protein: 5g | Fat: 9g | Fiber: 6g

Spinach and Feta Stuffed Peppers

Preparation Time: 10 minutes | **Cooking Time:** 25 minutes | **Servings:** 2

- **Ingredients**:

  1. 2 large bell peppers, tops removed, and seeds cleaned out
  2. 1/2 cup cooked spinach
  3. 1/4 cup crumbled feta cheese
  4. 1/4 cup cooked quinoa
  5. 1 tablespoon olive oil

- **Instructions**:

  1. Preheat the oven to 375°F (190°C).
  2. Mix spinach, quinoa, and feta cheese. Stuff the bell peppers with the mixture.
  3. Drizzle with olive oil and bake for 25 minutes.

- **Nutritional Information (per serving):**

Calories: 320 | Carbohydrates: 40g | Protein: 12g | Fat: 14g | Fiber: 10g

Eggplant Parmesan

Preparation Time: 15 minutes | **Cooking Time:** 30 minutes | **Servings:** 2

- **Ingredients:**

1. 1 large eggplant, sliced into rounds
2. 1/2 cup marinara sauce
3. 1/4 cup shredded mozzarella
4. 1 tablespoon Parmesan cheese
5. 1 tablespoon olive oil

- **Instructions:**

1. Preheat the oven to 375°F (190°C).
2. Brush eggplant slices with olive oil and roast for 20 minutes.
3. Top with marinara sauce, mozzarella, and Parmesan cheese, and bake for an additional 10 minutes until cheese is melted.

- **Nutritional Information (per serving):**

Calories: 280 | Carbohydrates: 24g | Protein: 12g | Fat: 16g | Fiber: 8g

Avocado and Chickpea Toast

Preparation Time: 5 minutes | **Cooking Time:** None | **Servings:** 1

- **Ingredients:**

  1. 1 slice whole-grain bread
  2. 1/4 avocado, mashed
  3. 1/4 cup chickpeas, mashed
  4. 1 tablespoon lemon juice
  5. Salt and pepper to taste

- **Instructions:**

  1. Toast the whole-grain bread.
  2. Mash chickpeas and avocado together, stir in lemon juice, salt, and pepper.
  3. Spread the mixture on toast and serve.

- **Nutritional Information:**

Calories: 240 | Carbohydrates: 30g | Protein: 8g | Fat: 12g | Fiber: 10g

Vegan Diet

A **vegan diet** excludes all animal products, including meat, dairy, and eggs. While this requires careful planning to ensure adequate protein intake, a well-rounded vegan diet can provide plenty of energy through plant-based whole foods.

Key Nutrients to Focus On:

- **Protein**: Include beans, lentils, tofu, tempeh, quinoa, and seitan as your main protein sources.
- **Calcium**: Incorporate calcium-fortified plant milks, tofu, and leafy greens.
- **Vitamin B12**: Like vegetarians, vegans should consider B12-fortified foods or supplements.

Recipes

Quinoa and Black Bean Bowl

Preparation Time: 10 minutes | **Cooking Time:** 10 minutes | **Servings:** 1

- **Ingredients**:

  1. 1/2 cup cooked quinoa
  2. 1/2 cup black beans, rinsed
  3. 1/4 cup cherry tomatoes, halved
  4. 1 tablespoon olive oil
  5. 1 tablespoon lime juice

- **Instructions**:

  1. Combine quinoa, black beans, and cherry tomatoes in a bowl.
  2. Drizzle with olive oil and lime juice, toss to combine, and serve.

- **Nutritional Information:**

  Calories: 320 | Carbohydrates: 42g | Protein: 12g | Fat: 12g | Fiber: 10g

Black Bean and Corn Salad

Preparation Time: 10 minutes | **Cooking Time:** None | **Servings:** 2

- **Ingredients**:

  1. 1/2 cup black beans, rinsed
  2. 1/2 cup corn (fresh or canned)
  3. 1/4 cup red bell pepper, diced
  4. 1/4 cup red onion, diced
  5. 1 tablespoon olive oil
  6. 1 tablespoon lime juice
  7. Salt and pepper to taste

- **Instructions**:

  1. In a bowl, combine black beans, corn, bell pepper, and onion.
  2. Drizzle with olive oil and lime juice, toss to combine.
  3. Season with salt and pepper and serve chilled.

- **Nutritional Information (per serving):**

  Calories: 220 | Carbohydrates: 40g | Protein: 7g | Fat: 6g | Fiber: 10g

Lentil Bolognese with Spaghetti

Preparation Time: 10 minutes | **Cooking Time:** 20 minutes | **Servings:** 2

- **Ingredients:**

  1. 1/2 cup dried lentils
  2. 1 cup marinara sauce
  3. 1/2 onion, diced
  4. 1 garlic clove, minced
  5. 1 tablespoon olive oil
  6. 1 cup spaghetti (use gluten-free or whole-wheat as desired)

- **Instructions:**

  1. Cook the spaghetti according to package instructions.
  2. While pasta cooks, heat olive oil in a pan and sauté onion and garlic until soft.
  3. Add lentils and marinara sauce, and simmer for 15 minutes until lentils are tender.
  4. Serve the lentil bolognese over the spaghetti.

- **Nutritional Information (per serving):**

Calories: 350 | Carbohydrates: 60g | Protein: 14g | Fat: 8g | Fiber: 12g

Vegan Buddha Bowl

Preparation Time: 10 minutes | **Cooking Time:** 10 minutes | **Servings:** 1

- **Ingredients:**

  1. 1/2 cup cooked quinoa
  2. 1/4 cup chickpeas, rinsed
  3. 1/4 cup roasted sweet potato
  4. 1/4 cup avocado, diced
  5. 1 tablespoon tahini
  6. 1 tablespoon lemon juice

- **Instructions:**

  1. In a bowl, layer quinoa, chickpeas, sweet potato, and avocado.
  2. Drizzle with tahini and lemon juice and toss to combine.

- **Nutritional Information:**

Calories: 320 | Carbohydrates: 40g | Protein: 10g | Fat: 14g | Fiber: 8g

Black Bean Burger

Preparation Time: 10 minutes | **Cooking Time:** 10 minutes | **Servings:** 2

- **Ingredients:**

  1. 1 can (15 oz) black beans, drained and rinsed
  2. 1/4 cup breadcrumbs (use gluten-free if needed)
  3. 1/4 cup onion, finely chopped
  4. 1 garlic clove, minced
  5. 1 tablespoon ground flaxseed mixed with 3 tablespoons water (flax egg)
  6. 1 teaspoon cumin
  7. 1 teaspoon smoked paprika
  8. 1 tablespoon olive oil (for cooking)
  9. Salt and pepper to taste
  10. Optional toppings: avocado slices, lettuce, tomato, vegan mayo, or ketchup
  11. 2 whole-grain or gluten-free buns

- **Instructions:**

  1. In a small bowl, mix the ground flaxseed with water and set aside for 5 minutes to thicken (this acts as a vegan egg substitute).
  2. In a large bowl, mash the black beans with a fork or potato masher until mostly smooth, leaving some chunks for texture.
  3. Add the chopped onion, minced garlic, cumin, smoked paprika, and the flax egg to the mashed black beans. Stir well.
  4. Gradually add the breadcrumbs and mix until the mixture holds together. Season with salt and pepper to taste.
  5. Divide the mixture into two equal portions and shape into patties.
  6. Heat olive oil in a skillet over medium heat and cook the patties for 4-5 minutes on each side, until golden and crispy.
  7. Serve the black bean burgers on buns with your favorite toppings like avocado, lettuce, tomato, and vegan mayo.

- **Nutritional Information (per burger with bun):**

  Calories: 350 | Carbohydrates: 50g | Protein: 15g | Fat: 10g | Fiber: 12g

Chickpea and Avocado Wrap

Preparation Time: 10 minutes | **Cooking Time:** None | **Servings:** 1

- **Ingredients:**

  1. 1 whole-wheat tortilla
  2. 1/4 cup mashed chickpeas
  3. 1/4 avocado, mashed

4. 1 tablespoon lemon juice
5. 1/4 cup spinach leaves

- **Instructions**:

    1. In a bowl, mash chickpeas and avocado together, and mix with lemon juice.
    2. Spread the mixture on the tortilla, top with spinach leaves, and roll it up.

- **Nutritional Information:**

Calories: 260 | Carbohydrates: 35g | Protein: 8g | Fat: 10g | Fiber: 10g

Spicy Black Bean Soup

Preparation Time: 10 minutes | **Cooking Time:** 20 minutes | **Servings:** 2

- **Ingredients**:

    1. 1 cup black beans, rinsed
    2. 1/2 onion, chopped
    3. 1 garlic clove, minced
    4. 1/2 teaspoon cumin
    5. 1/2 teaspoon chili powder
    6. 2 cups vegetable broth
    7. 1 tablespoon olive oil

- **Instructions**:

    1. Heat olive oil in a pot and sauté onion and garlic until soft.
    2. Add black beans, spices, and vegetable broth, and bring to a boil.
    3. Reduce heat and simmer for 15 minutes. Serve hot.

- **Nutritional Information (per serving):**

Calories: 250 | Carbohydrates: 40g | Protein: 10g | Fat: 8g | Fiber: 12g

Roasted Cauliflower Tacos

Preparation Time: 10 minutes | **Cooking Time:** 20 minutes | **Servings:** 2

- **Ingredients**:

    1. 1 small head of cauliflower, cut into florets
    2. 1 tablespoon olive oil

3. 1 teaspoon paprika
4. 1 tablespoon lime juice
5. 4 small corn tortillas
6. 1/4 cup salsa (optional)

- **Instructions**:

1. Preheat the oven to 400°F (200°C). Toss cauliflower florets with olive oil, paprika, and salt.
2. Roast for 20 minutes until tender.
3. Serve roasted cauliflower in tortillas, topped with lime juice and salsa.

- **Nutritional Information (per serving)**:

Calories: 280 | Carbohydrates: 45g | Protein: 6g | Fat: 10g | Fiber: 10g

Vegan Creamy Mushroom Risotto

Preparation Time: 10 minutes | **Cooking Time:** 20 minutes | **Servings:** 2

- **Ingredients**:

1. 1/2 cup arborio rice
2. 1 cup vegetable broth
3. 1/2 cup mushrooms, sliced
4. 1/4 cup onion, chopped
5. 1 tablespoon olive oil
6. 1 tablespoon nutritional yeast

- **Instructions**:

1. Heat olive oil in a pan and sauté onion and mushrooms until soft.
2. Add arborio rice and stir for 1-2 minutes. Gradually add vegetable broth, stirring constantly.
3. Cook for 15-20 minutes, adding broth as needed until rice is tender. Stir in nutritional yeast for a creamy finish.

- **Nutritional Information (per serving)**:

Calories: 320 | Carbohydrates: 55g | Protein: 7g | Fat: 10g | Fiber: 4g

Sweet Potato and Black Bean Enchiladas

Preparation Time: 10 minutes | **Cooking Time:** 20 minutes | **Servings:** 2

- **Ingredients:**

  1. 1 medium sweet potato, peeled and diced
  2. 1/2 cup black beans, rinsed
  3. 4 small corn tortillas
  4. 1/2 cup enchilada sauce
  5. 1 tablespoon olive oil

- **Instructions:**

  1. Preheat the oven to 375°F (190°C). Roast the sweet potato with olive oil for 20 minutes until tender.
  2. Fill tortillas with roasted sweet potatoes and black beans, roll them up, and place in a baking dish.
  3. Pour enchilada sauce over the tortillas and bake for 10 minutes.

- **Nutritional Information (per serving):**

Calories: 300 | Carbohydrates: 52g | Protein: 9g | Fat: 8g | Fiber: 12g

Gluten-Free Diet

A **gluten-free diet** is essential for those with celiac disease or gluten sensitivity. While gluten-containing grains like wheat, barley, and rye must be avoided, there are many gluten-free whole grains and starches that provide energy.

Key Nutrients to Focus On:

- **Fiber**: Ensure you're getting enough fiber from gluten-free grains like quinoa, brown rice, and oats (certified gluten-free).
- **B Vitamins**: These are often found in fortified grains, so look for gluten-free options that are enriched.
- **Iron**: Include leafy greens, lentils, and seeds for iron intake.

Recipes

Grilled Chicken and Quinoa Salad

Preparation Time: 10 minutes | **Cooking Time:** 10 minutes | **Servings:** 1

- **Ingredients:**

  1. 3 oz grilled chicken breast, sliced
  2. 1/2 cup cooked quinoa
  3. 1/4 cup cucumber, diced
  4. 1 tablespoon olive oil
  5. 1 tablespoon balsamic vinegar

- **Instructions:**

  1. In a bowl, combine the grilled chicken, quinoa, and cucumber.
  2. Drizzle with olive oil and balsamic vinegar, toss to combine, and serve.

- **Nutritional Information:**

Calories: 350 | Carbohydrates: 28g | Protein: 30g | Fat: 14g | Fiber: 6g

Quinoa and Roasted Vegetable Salad

Preparation Time: 10 minutes | **Cooking Time:** 25 minutes | **Servings:** 2

- **Ingredients:**

  1. 1/2 cup quinoa, cooked
  2. 1/2 cup zucchini, diced
  3. 1/2 cup bell peppers, diced
  4. 1/4 cup cherry tomatoes, halved
  5. 1 tablespoon olive oil
  6. 1 tablespoon balsamic vinegar
  7. Salt and pepper to taste

- **Instructions:**

  1. Preheat the oven to 400°F (200°C).
  2. Toss zucchini and bell peppers with olive oil and roast for 20-25 minutes until tender.
  3. In a bowl, combine cooked quinoa, roasted vegetables, and cherry tomatoes.
  4. Drizzle with balsamic vinegar, season with salt and pepper, and serve.

- **Nutritional Information (per serving:**

Calories: 300 | Carbohydrates: 40g | Protein: 8g | Fat: 12g | Fiber: 7g

Chicken and Sweet Potato Skillet

Preparation Time: 10 minutes | **Cooking Time:** 20 minutes | **Servings:** 1

- **Ingredients:**

  1. 3 oz chicken breast, diced
  2. 1 small, sweet potato, diced
  3. 1/2 cup spinach, chopped
  4. 1 tablespoon olive oil
  5. 1/2 teaspoon paprika
  6. Salt and pepper to taste

- **Instructions:**

  1. Heat olive oil in a skillet over medium heat and sauté the diced sweet potatoes for 8-10 minutes until tender.
  2. Add diced chicken and cook until browned and cooked through.
  3. Stir in spinach and cook until wilted. Season with paprika, salt, and pepper, and serve.

- **Nutritional Information:**

Calories: 320 | Carbohydrates: 30g | Protein: 25g | Fat: 12g | Fiber: 6g

Gluten-Free Veggie Stir-Fry

Preparation Time: 10 minutes | **Cooking Time:** 10 minutes | **Servings:** 1

- **Ingredients:**

  1. 1/2 cup broccoli florets
  2. 1/4 cup bell peppers, sliced
  3. 1/4 cup carrots, sliced
  4. 1 tablespoon gluten-free soy sauce
  5. 1 tablespoon olive oil
  6. 1/4 teaspoon ginger, minced

- **Instructions:**

  1. Heat olive oil in a pan and sauté broccoli, bell peppers, carrots, and ginger for 5-7 minutes.
  2. Stir in gluten-free soy sauce and cook for another 2-3 minutes. Serve hot.

- **Nutritional Information:**

Calories: 180 | Carbohydrates: 18g | Protein: 4g | Fat: 12g | Fiber: 6g

Stuffed Bell Peppers with Turkey and Quinoa

Preparation Time: 10 minutes | **Cooking Time:** 30 minutes | **Servings:** 2

- **Ingredients:**

  1. 2 large bell peppers, tops removed, and seeds cleaned out
  2. 1/2 cup cooked quinoa
  3. 3 oz ground turkey
  4. 1/4 cup onion, chopped
  5. 1 tablespoon olive oil
  6. 1 tablespoon tomato sauce

- **Instructions:**

  1. Preheat the oven to 375°F (190°C).
  2. In a skillet, cook the ground turkey and onion with olive oil until browned.
  3. Mix the cooked turkey with quinoa and tomato sauce, and stuff the bell peppers with the mixture.
  4. Bake for 30 minutes until the peppers are tender.

- **Nutritional Information (per serving):**

  Calories: 350 | Carbohydrates: 30g | Protein: 25g | Fat: 14g | Fiber: 8g

Gluten-Free Oatmeal Pancakes

Preparation Time: 5 minutes | **Cooking Time:** 10 minutes | **Servings:** 2

- **Ingredients:**

  1. 1/2 cup gluten-free oats
  2. 1/2 banana, mashed
  3. 1/4 cup almond milk
  4. 1 tablespoon chia seeds
  5. 1 teaspoon baking powder

- **Instructions:**

  1. Blend the oats into a fine flour consistency.
  2. Mix the oat flour with mashed banana, almond milk, chia seeds, and baking powder.
  3. Cook in a skillet over medium heat for 2-3 minutes on each side until golden brown.

- **Nutritional Information (per serving):**

  Calories: 220 | Carbohydrates: 36g | Protein: 5g | Fat: 6g | Fiber: 8g

Gluten-Free Chickpea Salad

Preparation Time: 10 minutes | **Cooking Time:** None | **Servings:** 1

- **Ingredients:**

  1. 1/2 cup canned chickpeas, rinsed
  2. 1/4 cup cucumber, diced
  3. 1/4 cup cherry tomatoes, halved
  4. 1 tablespoon olive oil
  5. 1 tablespoon lemon juice
  6. Salt and pepper to taste

- **Instructions:**

  1. In a bowl, combine chickpeas, cucumber, and cherry tomatoes.
  2. Drizzle with olive oil and lemon juice, toss to combine, and season with salt and pepper.

- **Nutritional Information:**

  Calories: 240 | Carbohydrates: 30g | Protein: 8g | Fat: 12g | Fiber: 8g

Baked Salmon with Asparagus

Preparation Time: 10 minutes | **Cooking Time:** 20 minutes | **Servings:** 1

- **Ingredients:**

  1. 4 oz salmon fillet
  2. 1/2 bunch asparagus, trimmed
  3. 1 tablespoon olive oil
  4. 1 tablespoon lemon juice
  5. Salt and pepper to taste

- **Instructions:**

  1. Preheat the oven to 375°F (190°C).
  2. Toss the asparagus with olive oil, salt, and pepper, and place on a baking sheet.
  3. Place the salmon fillet next to the asparagus, drizzle with lemon juice, and bake for 20 minutes.

- **Nutritional Information:**

  Calories: 350 | Carbohydrates: 8g | Protein: 28g | Fat: 24g | Fiber: 4g

Gluten-Free Falafel

Preparation Time: 10 minutes | **Cooking Time:** 20 minutes | **Servings:** 2

- **Ingredients:**

  1. 1 cup canned chickpeas, rinsed
  2. 1/4 cup onion, chopped
  3. 1 garlic clove, minced
  4. 2 tablespoons gluten-free flour (like chickpea flour)
  5. 1 tablespoon parsley, chopped
  6. 1 tablespoon olive oil

- **Instructions:**

  1. Blend chickpeas, onion, garlic, flour, and parsley in a food processor until combined but still slightly chunky.
  2. Form the mixture into small patties.
  3. Heat olive oil in a pan and fry the patties for 3-4 minutes on each side until golden brown.

- **Nutritional Information (per serving):**

  Calories: 280 | Carbohydrates: 36g | Protein: 10g | Fat: 12g | Fiber: 10g

Gluten-Free Chickpea Flour Pancakes

Preparation Time: 10 minutes | **Cooking Time:** 10 minutes | **Serving Size:** 2

- **Ingredients:**

  1. 1/2 cup chickpea flour (also known as gram flour)
  2. 1/2 cup water
  3. 1 tablespoon olive oil
  4. 1/4 teaspoon baking powder
  5. 1/4 teaspoon turmeric (optional for color)
  6. Salt and pepper to taste
  7. 1 tablespoon chopped fresh herbs (parsley, cilantro, or chives)
  8. 1/4 cup finely chopped vegetables (such as spinach, onions, or bell peppers) – optional

- **Instructions:**

  1. In a mixing bowl, whisk together the chickpea flour, water, olive oil, baking powder, turmeric (if using), salt, and pepper until smooth. Let the batter rest for 5 minutes to thicken.
  2. Stir in the chopped herbs and vegetables, if using, to add flavor and texture.
  3. Heat a non-stick skillet over medium heat and lightly grease with a little olive oil.
  4. Pour half of the batter into the skillet and spread it evenly to form a pancake. Cook for about 3-4 minutes on each side, until golden brown and firm. Repeat with the remaining batter.

5. Serve hot with a side of salad, avocado slices, or your favorite gluten-free sauce.

- **Nutritional Information (per serving):**

Calories: 200 | Carbohydrates: 22g | Protein: 8g | Fat: 8g | Fiber: 5g

Low-Carb Diet

A **low-carb or keto diet** focuses on reducing carbohydrate intake to encourage the body to burn fat for energy. While these diets often lead to rapid weight loss and increased energy, it's essential to ensure that you're still getting enough fiber and nutrients from non-starchy vegetables.

Key Nutrients to Focus On:

- **Healthy Fats**: Avocados, olive oil, nuts, seeds, and fatty fish provide essential fats for energy.
- **Fiber**: Since carbs are limited, focus on low-carb, fiber-rich vegetables like leafy greens, broccoli, and cauliflower.
- **Electrolytes**: It's important to get enough sodium, potassium, and magnesium to avoid the "keto flu."

Recipes

Avocado and Shrimp Salad

Preparation Time: 5 minutes | **Cooking Time:** 5 minutes | **Servings:** 1

- **Ingredients**:

  1. 4 oz shrimp, peeled and deveined
  2. 1/2 avocado, diced
  3. 1/4 cup cherry tomatoes, halved
  4. 1 tablespoon olive oil
  5. 1 tablespoon lime juice

- **Instructions**:

  1. Cook the shrimp in olive oil for 3-5 minutes until pink and fully cooked.
  2. Toss shrimp with avocado and cherry tomatoes in a bowl.
  3. Drizzle with lime juice and serve.

- **Nutritional Information:**

Calories: 300 | Carbohydrates: 10g | Protein: 25g | Fat: 20g | Fiber: 7g

Cauliflower Rice Stir-Fry with Shrimp

Preparation Time: 10 minutes | **Cooking Time:** 10 minutes | **Servings:** 1

- **Ingredients**:

  1. 1/2 cup cauliflower rice
  2. 4 oz shrimp, peeled and deveined
  3. 1/4 cup bell peppers, diced
  4. 1 tablespoon olive oil
  5. 1 tablespoon soy sauce (low-sodium)

- **Instructions**:

  1. Heat olive oil in a pan and sauté shrimp until pink, about 3-4 minutes.
  2. Add bell peppers and cauliflower rice, stir-frying for another 5 minutes.
  3. Stir in soy sauce and cook for 1-2 minutes more. Serve hot.

- **Nutritional Information:**

Calories: 240 | Carbohydrates: 8g | Protein: 25g | Fat: 12g | Fiber: 4g

Egg and Spinach Muffins

Preparation Time: 10 minutes | **Cooking Time:** 20 minutes | **Servings:** 2 (makes 6 muffins)

- **Ingredients:**

  1. 4 eggs
  2. 1/2 cup spinach, chopped
  3. 1/4 cup bell pepper, diced
  4. 1 tablespoon olive oil
  5. Salt and pepper to taste

- **Instructions:**

  1. Preheat the oven to 350°F (175°C).
  2. In a bowl, beat the eggs and stir in chopped spinach and bell pepper. Season with salt and pepper.
  3. Grease a muffin tin with olive oil and pour the egg mixture evenly into six cups.
  4. Bake for 15-20 minutes until fully set.

- **Nutritional Information (per serving):**

  Calories: 220 | Carbohydrates: 4g | Protein: 16g | Fat: 16g | Fiber: 2g

Avocado and Tuna Salad

Preparation Time: 5 minutes | **Cooking Time:** None | **Servings:** 1

- **Ingredients:**

  1. 1 can tuna in water, drained
  2. 1/2 avocado, mashed
  3. 1 tablespoon olive oil
  4. 1 tablespoon lemon juice
  5. Salt and pepper to taste

- **Instructions:**

  1. In a bowl, combine tuna, mashed avocado, olive oil, and lemon juice.
  2. Season with salt and pepper and serve immediately.

- **Nutritional Information:**

  Calories: 320 | Carbohydrates: 4g | Protein: 25g | Fat: 22g | Fiber: 5g

Grilled Salmon with Asparagus

Preparation Time: 10 minutes | **Cooking Time:** 15 minutes | **Servings:** 1

- **Ingredients:**

  1. 4 oz salmon fillet
  2. 1/2 bunch asparagus, trimmed
  3. 1 tablespoon olive oil
  4. 1 tablespoon lemon juice
  5. Salt and pepper to taste

- **Instructions:**

  1. Preheat grill to medium heat.
  2. Drizzle salmon and asparagus with olive oil and lemon juice, and season with salt and pepper.
  3. Grill salmon for 10-12 minutes until cooked through, and grill asparagus for 5-7 minutes until tender.

- **Nutritional Information:**

  Calories: 360 | Carbohydrates: 8g | Protein: 28g | Fat: 24g | Fiber: 5g

Turkey Lettuce Wraps

Preparation Time: 5 minutes | **Cooking Time:** 5 minutes | **Servings:** 1

- **Ingredients:**

  1. 3 oz ground turkey
  2. 1/4 cup bell peppers, diced
  3. 1 tablespoon soy sauce (low-sodium)
  4. 1 tablespoon olive oil
  5. 2 large lettuce leaves

- **Instructions:**

  1. Heat olive oil in a pan and cook ground turkey until browned.
  2. Add diced bell peppers and soy sauce and cook for another 2-3 minutes.
  3. Spoon the turkey mixture into lettuce leaves and serve.

- **Nutritional Information:**

  Calories: 240 | Carbohydrates: 6g | Protein: 25g | Fat: 12g | Fiber: 2g

Cauliflower Mashed "Potatoes"

Preparation Time: 10 minutes | **Cooking Time:** 10 minutes | **Servings:** 2

- **Ingredients:**

  1. 1 medium head of cauliflower, chopped
  2. 2 tablespoons olive oil
  3. 2 tablespoons almond milk (unsweetened)
  4. Salt and pepper to taste

- **Instructions:**

  1. Steam the cauliflower for 8-10 minutes until tender.
  2. In a food processor, blend steamed cauliflower with olive oil and almond milk until smooth.
  3. Season with salt and pepper and serve as a low-carb side dish.

- **Nutritional Information (per serving):**

Calories: 150 | Carbohydrates: 8g | Protein: 3g | Fat: 12g | Fiber: 4g

Creamy Garlic Shrimp

Preparation Time: 10 minutes | **Cooking Time:** 10 minutes | **Servings:** 1

- **Ingredients:**

  1. 4 oz shrimp, peeled and deveined
  2. 1/4 cup coconut cream (or heavy cream)
  3. 1 garlic clove, minced
  4. 1 tablespoon olive oil
  5. 1 tablespoon fresh parsley, chopped
  6. Salt and pepper to taste

- **Instructions:**

  1. Heat olive oil in a pan over medium heat and sauté minced garlic until fragrant.
  2. Add shrimp and cook for 3-4 minutes until pink.
  3. Pour in the coconut cream, season with salt and pepper, and let it simmer for 2-3 minutes until the sauce thickens.
  4. Garnish with fresh parsley and serve hot.

- **Nutritional Information:**

Calories: 320 | Carbohydrates: 4g | Protein: 22g | Fat: 24g | Fiber: 1g

Baked Eggs in Avocado

Preparation Time: 5 minutes | **Cooking Time:** 15 minutes | **Servings:** 1

- **Ingredients:**

  1. 1 large avocado, halved and pit removed
  2. 2 small eggs
  3. Salt and pepper to taste
  4. 1 tablespoon chopped chives or parsley (optional)

- **Instructions:**

  1. Preheat the oven to 350°F (175°C).
  2. Scoop out a little more of the avocado flesh to create room for the eggs.
  3. Crack an egg into each avocado half, season with salt and pepper, and place in a baking dish.
  4. Bake for 12-15 minutes or until the eggs are cooked to your liking.
  5. Garnish with chopped chives or parsley before serving.

- **Nutritional Information:**

  Calories: 300 | Carbohydrates: 10g | Protein: 12g | Fat: 26g | Fiber: 7g

Cheesy Cauliflower Bake

Preparation Time: 10 minutes | **Cooking Time:** 20 minutes | **Servings:** 2

- **Ingredients:**

  1. 1 medium head of cauliflower, chopped into florets
  2. 1/2 cup shredded cheddar cheese (or your preferred cheese)
  3. 1/4 cup heavy cream
  4. 1 tablespoon olive oil
  5. 1 garlic clove, minced
  6. Salt and pepper to taste
  7. 1 tablespoon fresh parsley, chopped (optional)

- **Instructions:**

  1. Preheat the oven to 375°F (190°C).
  2. Steam or boil cauliflower florets until tender (about 5-7 minutes).
  3. In a skillet, heat olive oil and sauté minced garlic until fragrant.
  4. Add the cooked cauliflower to the skillet, stirring in the heavy cream and shredded cheese. Mix until cheese is melted, and cauliflower is coated.
  5. Transfer the cauliflower mixture to a baking dish, season with salt and pepper, and bake for 10-12 minutes, or until the top is golden and bubbly.

6. Garnish with chopped parsley before serving, if desired.

- **Nutritional Information:**

Calories: 320 | Carbohydrates: 10g | Protein: 12g | Fat: 28g | Fiber: 4g

Chapter 9: Quick Recipes for Busy Days

In today's fast-paced world, finding time to prepare nutritious, balanced meals can feel like a challenge. But being busy doesn't mean you have to sacrifice healthy eating or resort to processed, convenience foods that leave you feeling sluggish. With the right quick and easy recipes, you can fuel your body with energizing meals that come together in minutes, keeping you nourished and focused even on your busiest days.

Whether you're rushing out the door in the morning, need a quick lunch, or are looking for a speedy dinner after a long day, these recipes are designed to fit seamlessly into your busy schedule.

Why Quick Meals Matter for Energy

When you're pressed for time, it can be tempting to reach for processed foods, sugary snacks, or fast food that provide quick bursts of energy but leave you crashing soon after. Quick meals made with whole, nutrient-dense ingredients help keep your blood sugar stable, providing sustained energy throughout the day. They are packed with the right balance of complex carbohydrates, lean proteins, and healthy fats to keep you satisfied and energized, no matter how busy your day gets.

Quick meals don't have to be complicated. With just a few simple ingredients and a little planning, you can whip up meals that are both satisfying and packed with nutrients.

Quick and Energizing Recipes

Here are 10 delicious, nutritious meals that can be prepared in 30 minutes or less perfect for busy days when you need something quick but don't want to compromise on health or taste.

Chicken and Quinoa Bowl

Preparation Time: 10 minutes | **Cooking Time:** 10 minutes | **Servings:** 1

- **Ingredients:**

  1. 3 oz grilled chicken breast, sliced
  2. 1/2 cup cooked quinoa
  3. 1/4 cup cherry tomatoes, halved
  4. 1/4 cup cucumber, diced
  5. 1 tablespoon olive oil
  6. 1 tablespoon lemon juice

- **Instructions:**

  1. In a bowl, combine the cooked quinoa, grilled chicken, cherry tomatoes, and cucumber.
  2. Drizzle with olive oil and lemon juice, toss to combine, and serve.

- **Nutritional Information:**

Calories: 320 | Carbohydrates: 28g | Protein: 30g | Fat: 12g | Fiber: 5g

Quick Veggie Frittata

Preparation Time: 5 minutes | **Cooking Time:** 10 minutes | **Servings:** 1

- **Ingredients:**

  1. 2 eggs
  2. 1/4 cup spinach, chopped
  3. 1/4 cup bell peppers, diced
  4. 1 tablespoon olive oil
  5. Salt and pepper to taste

- **Instructions:**

  1. Heat olive oil in a small skillet and sauté the bell peppers and spinach until soft.
  2. In a bowl, beat the eggs with salt and pepper, then pour over the veggies in the skillet.
  3. Cook for 5-7 minutes until the eggs are fully set. Serve hot.

- **Nutritional Information:**

Calories: 240 | Carbohydrates: 5g | Protein: 14g | Fat: 18g | Fiber: 2g

Veggie Stir-Fry with Tofu

Preparation Time: 10 minutes | **Cooking Time:** 10 minutes | **Servings:** 1

- **Ingredients:**

  1. 1/2 block tofu, cubed
  2. 1 cup mixed vegetables (broccoli, bell peppers, carrots)
  3. 1 tablespoon soy sauce
  4. 1 tablespoon olive oil

- **Instructions**:

  1. Heat olive oil in a pan and stir-fry tofu until golden.
  2. Add mixed vegetables and soy sauce, cooking for 5-7 minutes.
  3. Serve hot.

- **Nutritional Information**:

Calories: 250 | Carbohydrates: 16g | Protein: 14g | Fat: 14g | Fiber: 5g

Chicken and Avocado Salad

Preparation Time: 10 minutes | **Cooking Time:** None | **Servings:** 1

- **Ingredients**:

  1. 1 cup mixed greens
  2. 1/2 avocado, diced
  3. 3 oz grilled chicken breast, sliced
  4. 1 tablespoon olive oil
  5. 1 tablespoon balsamic vinegar

- **Instructions**:

  1. In a bowl, toss mixed greens, avocado, and grilled chicken.
  2. Drizzle with olive oil and balsamic vinegar and serve.

- **Nutritional Information**:

Calories: 300 | Carbohydrates: 8g | Protein: 25g | Fat: 18g | Fiber: 6g

Cucumber and Hummus Sandwich

Preparation Time: 5 minutes | **Cooking Time:** None | **Servings:** 1

- **Ingredients**:

  1. 2 slices gluten-free bread or whole-grain bread
  2. 2 tablespoons hummus (store-bought or homemade)
  3. 1/4 cucumber, thinly sliced
  4. 1 tablespoon fresh parsley, chopped (optional)
  5. 1 tablespoon olive oil (optional for drizzling)
  6. Salt and pepper to taste

- **Instructions:**

  1. Spread 1 tablespoon of hummus on each slice of bread.
  2. Layer the cucumber slices evenly on one slice.
  3. Sprinkle with fresh parsley, salt, and pepper. Drizzle olive oil on top if desired.
  4. Place the other slice of bread on top to make a sandwich and enjoy immediately.

- **Nutritional Information:**

Calories: 280 | Carbohydrates: 42g | Protein: 8g | Fat: 10g | Fiber: 7g

Tuna Salad Lettuce Wraps

Preparation Time: 5 minutes | **Cooking Time:** None | **Servings:** 1

- **Ingredients:**

  1. 1 can tuna in water, drained
  2. 1 tablespoon Greek yogurt
  3. 1/4 avocado, diced
  4. 1/4 cup cucumber, diced
  5. 2 large lettuce leaves

- **Instructions:**

  1. In a bowl, mix the tuna, Greek yogurt, avocado, and cucumber.
  2. Spoon the mixture into lettuce leaves and serve as wraps.

- **Nutritional Information:**

Calories: 220 | Carbohydrates: 6g | Protein: 25g | Fat: 10g | Fiber: 4g

Shrimp Tacos with Avocado

Preparation Time: 10 minutes | **Cooking Time:** 10 minutes | **Servings:** 2

- **Ingredients:**

  1. 4 oz shrimp, peeled and deveined
  2. 2 corn tortillas
  3. 1/4 avocado, sliced
  4. 1 tablespoon lime juice
  5. 1 tablespoon olive oil

- **Instructions**:

    1. Heat olive oil in a pan and cook shrimp for 5-7 minutes.
    2. Serve shrimp in tortillas with avocado slices and a drizzle of lime juice.

- **Nutritional Information:**

Calories: 280 | Carbohydrates: 20g | Protein: 20g | Fat: 12g | Fiber: 4g

Spicy Shrimp and Avocado Salad

Preparation Time: 5 minutes | **Cooking Time:** 5 minutes | **Servings:** 1

- **Ingredients:**

    1. 4 oz shrimp, peeled and deveined
    2. 1/2 avocado, diced
    3. 1/4 cup cherry tomatoes, halved
    4. 1 tablespoon olive oil
    5. 1 tablespoon lime juice
    6. 1/2 teaspoon chili powder
    7. Salt and pepper to taste

- **Instructions:**

    1. Heat olive oil in a pan and cook the shrimp for 3-5 minutes, until pink and fully cooked.
    2. In a bowl, combine avocado, cherry tomatoes, and cooked shrimp.
    3. Drizzle with lime juice, sprinkle with chili powder, and season with salt and pepper. Toss gently and serve.

- **Nutritional Information:**

Calories: 300 | Carbohydrates: 10g | Protein: 25g | Fat: 20g | Fiber: 7g

Whole-Grain Pasta with Pesto

Preparation Time: 5 minutes | **Cooking Time:** 10 minutes | **Servings:** 2

- **Ingredients:**

  1. 1 cup whole-grain pasta
  2. 2 tablespoons pesto
  3. 1 tablespoon olive oil

- **Instructions:**

  1. Cook the whole-grain pasta according to package instructions.
  2. Drain and toss with pesto and olive oil.
  3. Serve hot.

- **Nutritional Information:**

  Calories: 320 | Carbohydrates: 40g | Protein: 10g | Fat: 14g | Fiber: 6g

Turkey and Hummus Wrap

Preparation Time: 5 minutes | **Cooking Time:** None | **Servings:** 1

- **Ingredients:**

  1. 1 whole-wheat tortilla
  2. 2 oz sliced turkey breast
  3. 2 tablespoons hummus
  4. 1/4 cup spinach leaves

- **Instructions:**

  1. Spread hummus on the tortilla, add turkey slices and spinach.
  2. Roll up the tortilla and serve immediately.

- **Nutritional Information:**

  Calories: 250 | Carbohydrates: 24g | Protein: 18g | Fat: 10g | Fiber: 4g

Chapter 10: Detox Plan

Our bodies are designed to naturally detoxify and cleanse, but sometimes, due to the buildup of toxins from processed foods, stress, or environmental pollutants, they can use a little extra support. A well-balanced detox plan helps reset your system by focusing on whole, nutrient-dense foods that support your body's natural detox processes. Rather than resorting to extreme cleanses or restrictive diets, this detox plan is based on nourishing your body with healthy foods that promote digestion, hydration, and overall well-being.

In this chapter, you'll find a simple, effective detox plan that uses clean, whole foods to boost your energy, improve digestion, and leave you feeling refreshed and revitalized. These recipes are designed to be gentle on your system while providing all the nutrients your body needs to function at its best.

Why Detox Matters for Energy and Wellness

Detoxing helps your body eliminate toxins and rejuvenate, making it easier for you to maintain consistent energy levels, mental clarity, and optimal health. A detox doesn't have to be a restrictive or difficult process—it's about giving your body a break from processed foods, refined sugars, and artificial ingredients. By focusing on whole foods like fruits, vegetables, and healthy fats, you're nourishing your body and supporting its natural detox pathways.

Key benefits of a detox plan include:

- **Improved Digestion**: A detox can help reset your digestive system by including foods that are rich in fiber and water, which aid in flushing out toxins.
- **Increased Energy**: By avoiding processed foods and focusing on nutrient-dense options, your energy levels will stabilize, and you'll avoid the highs and lows that come with sugar crashes.
- **Better Skin and Mental Clarity**: A clean diet filled with antioxidants and hydration can improve skin health and reduce brain fog, leaving you feeling and looking refreshed.

Key Detox Foods

When following a detox plan, it's important to focus on foods that support your body's natural cleansing processes. Here are some of the key ingredients to include:

1. **Leafy Greens**
   o Rich in vitamins, minerals, and chlorophyll, which help detoxify the liver and improve digestion.
   o **Examples**: Spinach, kale, Swiss chard, and arugula.
2. **Citrus Fruits**
   o High in vitamin C and antioxidants, which aid in the detoxification process and boost the immune system.

- Examples: Lemons, limes, oranges, and grapefruits.
3. **Cruciferous Vegetables**
    - Packed with fiber and sulfur compounds that help flush out toxins and promote liver health.
    - **Examples**: Broccoli, cauliflower, cabbage, and Brussels sprouts.
4. **Ginger and Turmeric**
    - Known for their anti-inflammatory properties, these spices can support digestion and reduce bloating.
    - **Examples**: Fresh ginger root and ground turmeric.
5. **Hydrating Foods**
    - Foods high in water content help flush out toxins and keep you hydrated.
    - **Examples**: Cucumbers, watermelon, celery, and leafy greens.
6. **Healthy Fats**
    - Healthy fats support liver function and help absorb fat-soluble vitamins.
    - **Examples**: Avocados, nuts, seeds, and olive oil.

Detox Plan Guidelines

For a simple detox, aim to follow these guidelines for 3-5 days:

1. Focus on whole, unprocessed foods.
2. Drink plenty of water, herbal teas, and detoxifying beverages like lemon water.
3. Avoid refined sugars, processed foods, caffeine, alcohol, and excessive salt.
4. Include plenty of fresh fruits, vegetables, lean proteins, and healthy fats.
5. Get adequate rest and try to incorporate light exercise or stretching.

3-Day Detox Plan

Day 1:

- **Morning**:

Lemon Water Detox Drink

- 1 cup warm water with the juice of 1/2 lemon.

Green Detox Smoothie

- 1 cup spinach
- 1/2 banana
- 1/2 cup cucumber
- 1 tablespoon chia seeds

o   1 cup unsweetened almond milk

Blend all ingredients together and enjoy.

- **Lunch:**

  Kale and Quinoa Salad

  o   1/2 cup cooked quinoa
  o   1 cup chopped kale
  o   1/4 avocado
  o   1 tablespoon olive oil
  o   1 tablespoon lemon juice

  Combine all ingredients and toss with olive oil and lemon juice.

- **Dinner:**

  Lentil and Vegetable Soup

  o   1/2 cup cooked lentils
  o   1 cup spinach
  o   1/2 cup diced carrots
  o   1/2 cup diced celery
  o   2 cups vegetable broth

  Simmer all ingredients for 20 minutes and serve.

Day 2:

- **Morning:**

  Cucumber and Mint Water

  o   1 cup water with cucumber slices and fresh mint leaves.

  Avocado Toast with Egg

  o   1 slice whole-grain toast
  o   1/2 avocado, mashed
  o   1 poached egg

  Spread the mashed avocado on toast and top with the egg.

- **Lunch:**

Spinach and Chickpea Salad

- o 1 cup spinach
- o 1/2 cup chickpeas
- o 1/4 cup cherry tomatoes
- o 1 tablespoon olive oil

Toss all ingredients together and serve with olive oil.

- **Dinner:**

Grilled Salmon with Steamed Broccoli

- o 4 oz grilled salmon
- o 1 cup steamed broccoli
- o 1 tablespoon lemon juice

Grill the salmon and serve with broccoli, drizzled with lemon juice.

Day 3:

- **Morning:**

Lemon Water Detox Drink Turmeric Ginger Tea

- o 1 cup hot water
- o 1/2 teaspoon turmeric
- o 1/2 teaspoon grated ginger

Mix and sip for an anti-inflammatory boost.

Berry and Flaxseed Smoothie

- o 1 cup mixed berries
- o 1 tablespoon flaxseeds
- o 1 cup coconut water

Blend all ingredients together and enjoy.

- **Lunch:**

Cucumber and Avocado Salad

- o   1 cup diced cucumber
- o   1/4 avocado, diced
- o   1 tablespoon lemon juice
- o   1 tablespoon olive oil

Toss all ingredients together and serve.

- **Dinner:**

Zucchini Noodles with Pesto

- o   1 cup zucchini noodles (spiralized)
- o   2 tablespoons pesto (homemade or store-bought)

Toss zucchini noodles with pesto and serve.

Detox-Friendly Snacks

If you feel hungry between meals, here are a few detox-friendly snacks to keep you going:

- **Sliced Veggies with Hummus**
- **Apple Slices with Almond Butter**
- **Mixed Berries with Greek Yogurt**
- **Handful of Raw Nuts (almonds, walnuts, or cashews)**

Conclusion: Energize Your Life

You've made it to the end of **The Good Energy Cookbook**, but this is just the beginning of your journey to sustained energy and vibrant health. Throughout these pages, you've learned how the right foods can fuel your body, sharpen your mind, and keep you going all day long—without the crashes and fatigue that come from poor nutrition. Now it's time to take that knowledge and make it part of your everyday life.

The meals, snacks, and tips in this book are designed to fit seamlessly into your routine, no matter how busy you are. Whether you're looking to stay energized at work, fuel your workouts, or simply avoid that afternoon slump, the recipes here give you the tools to maintain steady energy and mental clarity. By choosing whole, nutrient-dense foods—like complex carbohydrates, lean proteins, and healthy fats—you can power your body the way it was meant to be fuelled.

But this journey isn't just about the food on your plate—it's about adopting a lifestyle that supports long-term health and vitality. As you experiment with these recipes and incorporate them into your routine, you'll find that eating for energy doesn't have to be complicated. In fact, it can be delicious, satisfying, and incredibly rewarding.

Here are a few final tips to help you continue on the path to sustained energy:

- **Listen to Your Body**: Pay attention to how different foods make you feel. Some meals will leave you feeling more energized than others. Use that feedback to refine your choices and discover what works best for your body.
- **Stay Hydrated**: Don't forget that water is an essential part of keeping your energy levels up. Aim to stay hydrated throughout the day to support digestion, brain function, and overall energy.
- **Be Consistent**: The benefits of a good energy diet build over time. Stick with these habits, and you'll notice improvements in your mood, focus, and physical stamina.
- **Enjoy the Process**: Cooking and eating should be enjoyable experiences. Experiment with new flavors, try different combinations, and have fun in the kitchen as you create meals that make you feel great.

The key to sustained energy isn't about perfection—it's about balance. By consistently choosing foods that fuel you, listening to your body, and making small adjustments as needed, you'll be well on your way to a life filled with energy, focus, and vitality.

Now it's time to take what you've learned and put it into action. Your energy, your health, and your future are all in your hands. Here's to feeling your best, every single day.

Energize your life, one meal at a time!

SCAN HERE TO DOWNLOAD THE BONUS

OR COPY AND PASTE THE URL

https://qrco.de/bfSPAV

Made in the USA
Coppell, TX
24 November 2024